Mr & Mrs
BUSINESS

HOW TO CREATE SUCCESS WITHOUT STRESS AS A COUPLE IN BUSINESS

SONJA BALZAROLO

First Edition. Published 2020
© Sonja Balzarolo 2020

Mr & Mrs Business – How to create success without stress as a couple in business

ISBN: Paperback: 978-0-6488422-0-0
ISBN: eBook ePUB: 978-0-6488422-1-7
ISBN: eBook pdf: 978-0-6488422-2-4

Publisher: Blossoming Business
Gold Coast, Australia

www.blossomingbusiness.com.au

For order information, specifically quantity sales and orders by trade bookstores or wholesalers, contact Sonja Balzarolo at sonja@blossomingbusiness.com.au.

Categories 1. Business 2. Finance, Personal
Author photograph: Annie Noon
Cover design: Emma Veiga-Malta
Edited by: Joanne Speirs

Blossoming Business

HELPING YOUR BUSINESS GROW

Dedication

This book is dedicated to my daughters,
Lily-Rose and LuLu Sparkle.

Thank you for giving me back the gift of creativity.

Contents

Preface

*B*efore we get to know each other and dive into Money, Time and Self-Care, there are a few things I felt it important to preface this book with.

Success Without Stress

It would be unfair of me to give you the idea that in reading this book and doing the suggested exercises, you'll 100% achieve success with absolutely no stress.

My intention in writing Mr & Mrs Business is to bring awareness to the importance managing your money, time and self-care plays in achieving success without stress as a couple in business. Awareness is the first step in reducing or removing the stress created by money and time issues (or the stress created by not having self-care). Bringing awareness allows you to implement changes that manage these critical business areas well.

You can achieve success without having the stress levels that are now affecting couples in business (and the world at large), with overwhelm, burnout and increasing health issues becoming commonplace. Can you achieve success without any stress? That's entirely in your hands. I'm a constant work in progress and success without stress is a daily goal.

This book is your guide to working towards success without stress. Let this be the goal you strive towards every day. Even getting close to achieving this can make a world of difference to your relationship and your business!

What This Book Isn't

You should know this isn't a marketing book, an instructional guide on how to grow your business, a book on how to make money or how to communicate better as a couple. It also isn't a counselling or relationship guidance book.

I don't give financial advice for your business or personal circumstances in this book, nor am I qualified to do so.

The disclaimer which you may have skipped past on page 2 reads: *This book and any associated materials, suggestions and advice are intended to give general information only. The author expressly disclaims all liability to any person arising directly or indirectly from the use of, or for any errors or omissions in this book. The adoption and application of the information in this book is at the readers' discretion and is his or her sole responsibility.*

Now that's out of the way, let's get started!

Introduction

Success for me is finding ways to bring creativity into my work and life, being organised and helping others. I thrive on the joy found in creating, advising, teaching, mentoring and organising.

My childhood memories are full of make-believe schools where I was always the teacher, running events with the neighbourhood kids and lots of creative endeavours.

And in my work now, I love helping business owners just like you by providing knowledge and clarity around your finances and business operations. I give you time to focus on the things you love in your business and advise you to take care of yourselves as well as your business.

My life experiences, skills and natural talents have all merged to create a business and a life that's fulfilling.

But this didn't happen by accident or overnight. In the last five years, I've purpose-built a business that aligns with my definition of success (without stress), honours my core values and will achieve my families shared vision for the future.

I've made many mistakes along the way and weathered many setbacks. But I've also had plenty of successful outcomes and priceless experiences. These have resulted in a set of essential business foundations focused on Money, Time and Self-Care that bring a unique value to my work in helping businesses grow.

Putting these foundations together in written form has allowed me to follow my own advice and pursue a long-held dream of writing a book.

I believe in self-discovery, understanding what the best version of you looks like and bringing it to life by sharing your talents and working on your dreams. It's a fascinating journey.

One of my earliest memories in childhood is from grade one. A Disney book with all the usual characters caught my attention and I decided to recreate the book into a concert. I recruited my classmates, planned who would play what role and assumed our parents would make all of the amazing costumes.

What I didn't plan for was the amount of work involved for the teachers and parents for my amazing production to come to life, and sadly, the concert didn't go ahead.

My early love of planning and organising built confidence and developed my ability to see the bigger picture, plan out an idea and take action.

I've always believed anything is possible. No dream was ever too big, and I tested this out many times. In 1999, aged twenty-seven, I quit a great job in Melbourne to travel the world solo. In 2001, I took on a role as General Manager for a large business in London, having never managed staff or worked in that industry (healthcare) before. In 2014, I left a six-figure corporate career behind, and having never worked for myself, created my business from scratch.

So why write a book about couples in business? I've been fortunate to work with a variety of businesses that have been couple or family-run. Through my work with these businesses, I've recognised three factors that commonly create stress and frustration and put limits on our success.

They are: Money, Time and Self-Care.

When we add being a couple in business, these three things go up a notch (or ten) and become even harder to manage.

I also recognised that these three factors were often the most neglected or hard to manage in a business (not always consciously).

A 2019 survey by Yellow of one hundred small business owners, reported the top stressors as managing business finances (32%), juggling multiple responsibilities (26%) and no work-life balance (16%). Half of those surveyed said they work more than nine hours per day — much higher than the daily average of seven point six working hours (Sensis 2019).

In this example, money, time and not prioritising self-care accounted for 74% of the stressors for small business owners.

I don't take this topic lightly. I know there are couples in business out there needing help. I know the statistics on businesses making it past year three are low (averaged at 64.5% by the The Australian Small Business and Family Enterprise Ombudman (ASBFEO) 2019).

But I believe in the foundations I'm sharing and the positive effect they can have on achieving a sustainable, profitable and successful business for couples.

As of June 30, 2019, there were 2.3 million actively trading businesses in the Australian economy, which is a 2.7% increase in businesses on the previous year (Australian Bureau of Statistics 2020).

If only 10% of those businesses (and I suspect it's much higher) were couple and family-run, then that's over 230,000 Australian businesses. According to the numbers by the ASBFEO report, if more than 35.5% of businesses close within the first three years, that indicates 81,650 of our estimated 230,000 couple and family-run businesses won't make it.

That's a scary statistic, and one I'd love to play a small part in reducing by addressing, in this book, the top three stressors for business owners today.

This book intends to provide simple things you can do straight away that will help you to:
- reduce stress and pressure in your working and family life
- feel satisfaction and success

- give you the motivation to spend some time on you in order to meet the vision you have for yourself, your partner and the business you're building together.

Finding the Fun in Business

Why did you start your business? Was it to create more freedom, money, flexibility, or fulfil a long-held dream? I'm going to take a guess and say that it wasn't to create stress, long hours, strain in your relationship, a lack of time to do things you enjoy or to feel defeated by the dollar.

Building a business with your partner should be an enjoyable, fulfilling experience. One that not only helps you achieve your shared vision as a family but one that gives you a sense of achievement, fulfilment and pride.

Your business is a shared adventure that can give you a new appreciation and love for the talents of your partner. It provides you with a space that's yours and encourages you to grow together and build something meaningful to you both. It's a means to have the freedom to control your earnings, your time, your independence, your workload and the future for your family.

As you build or refine your shared vision for your business as a couple, make sure you take this into consideration. Finding the fun in your business, and the joy of being in business together is essential. Your relationship is too precious for your time as a couple in business to be miserable. If this is the reality for you right now, use this book to get you back on track.

Who Is This Book For?

Mr & Mrs Business is for couples considering going into business together and couples already in business.

If you're at the 'considering' stage as a couple, you'll find tools to help you make an informed decision about whether you should move forward as a couple in business, and the important foundations to create as you begin your journey in business together.

If you're already a couple in business, you have the freedom to take action and pivot, revise or restructure whenever you please. This book will help you see your business and your relationship from a different viewpoint so you can take informed action in any areas that would benefit from a change.

How to Read This Book and What to Expect

Do you wish you could wave a magic wand and spend minimal time at work while making lots of money? Do you wish you had the perfect working relationship with your partner, and everything ran smoothly?

Chances are you won't achieve that with this book (hey, I'm no miracle worker!), but we can absolutely make a start on reducing your stress, give you some time back and create some space for you to take care of your needs and desires in business, and in life outside of your business.

Mr & Mrs Business is written in three sections – Money, Time and Self-Care.

Each section has information, an exercise to work through and ideas on how to create changes relating to that section's topic.

You can, of course, go straight to the section that appeals to you, but they've been created, so each section builds on the last and leads into the one following it.

At the end of the book, there's an additional resources section if you want to dive deeper into these topics via your own research.

This book has been written for couples in business, but with the understanding, it will likely be purchased by one part of the couple, read and then given to the other partner. Consider buying two books (a Mr and a Mrs copy!) and work through/read it together.

Important: This book also contains the Mr & Mrs Business Couples Quiz (found at the back of the book on page 141).

If you're not reading this book with your partner, it's a good idea to get him/her to complete the quiz before you get started. It'll give you some clarity on your current working relationship status and provide a little bit of light-hearted fun to create an open mindset as you work your way through the book. (It may also have the bonus of creating curiosity from your partner and inspire them to read the book with you.)

On a final note, before we get started, I sincerely hope my enthusiasm for helping you in your business can be felt through the pages of this book, and you sense my ongoing encouragement for you to find your version of success without stress as a couple in business.

Whether it's money, time or self-care you want more of, know that I'm here to support and cheer you on.

Sonja

FOUNDATIONS CHAPTER

Couples in Business

When I first decided to start a business, my husband John and I thought we'd set up a business together. It seemed to make good business sense. John is a qualified bookkeeper and BAS agent, and I was planning on building a support service business using the skills and experience gained from my corporate career.

From the outside, it looked like the right mix of our skills and a solid offering to our target clients – small business owners. And we could work from home, build a business together and share the workload, marketing, clients, etc.

I threw myself into setting up the business side of things – decided on a name, registered the business, set up social media and the website and started getting clients.

But within six months things weren't turning out as planned. I started thinking we'd made a bad decision and I found myself constantly thinking, 'I want out. This isn't what I imagined working together would be like.'

Now, when I look back on what went wrong, the gaps are obvious. We didn't invest the time to discuss our values, our goals for the business, how we would work and live together, how our family would fit into this (we had two and a half-year-old and nine-month-old children at the time), what boundaries we needed and who would be responsible for what. We had not created a shared vision for our future.

We ended up with differing opinions, stress, disorganisation and tension that spilled over into our family life. With such young children, this wasn't the time to be creating more stress for our family. So we decided to split our business, and I branched out into my own consultancy.

For a long time, I felt like we just weren't one of those couples who could work together. But as I started to develop my consultancy business, I took an interest in how other couples built their businesses, and in particular, what worked and what didn't in their partnership.

The realisation soon came it wasn't us or how we worked that was the issue. It was a lack of foundations based on minimal planning, no shared vision and direction and no conversations around the unique needs of working as a couple. We weren't working together as a couple in business but instead acting as owners of two separate businesses.

From this experience, I could see the important foundations we missed in our approach to setting up a business as a couple. I've seen similar foundations missing with clients.

In the following chapters, I want to share with you some of the simple money, time and self-care strategies you can use to avoid making the same mistakes. Strategies to help support you as you build the business you envision with your partner.

Conscious Business Coupling

When Gwyneth Paltrow and Chris Martin decided to 'consciously uncouple' in 2014, the world was divided by this so-called new-age explanation for what we know as divorce.

While I love a good 'find a new word for an old word' game, the concept of what Gwyneth and Chris announced to the world is, in fact, a great example for couples - make conscious decisions.

Being a couple in business can bring about many changes to your relationship, some positive and some not so much. Therefore, it makes sense to consciously decide to enter into business as a couple (or make some conscious changes as a couple in business).

By making conscious decisions armed with the right information and clarity on the implications of being business owners together, you give yourselves a great shot at success without stress.

This might seem like an unusual concept to some. It may seem logical to others. But the reality is the number of couples who enter into business together unconsciously, i.e. without thinking about the effect it will have on their marriage or partnership, is in my experience rather high. I've been there myself!

Conscious Business Coupling means taking into account all of the things that could affect you as a couple if you go into or are in business together and deciding if being a couple in business is worth it. Decide if the foundations you need to put in place are achievable, possible, and something you're prepared to work towards as a couple - because it does take work.

Creating a business as a couple often seems like the sensible thing to do. In the beginning, you envision the money you'll save on staffing by taking on a lot of the tasks yourselves. And it's important to point out that you won't find a more committed and passionate employee than you and your partner!

But it's equally important to view with eyes wide open the realities of being in business as a couple.

Let's Talk – Conscious Business Coupling Questions

There are questions you need to ask each other in order to achieve Conscious Business Coupling. Below you'll find some to get you started, but feel free to add your own.

Make some time to spend an hour or more together to discuss and either write down your answers or type them into a document on your computer. What you discover from asking these questions forms an important base to creating a shared vision.

1. Why are we going into, or why are we in business together?
2. How will we be/are we supporting each other in business?
3. What will be/are each of our hours of work? Will they differ or be the same for both of us? (Important especially if you have children.)
4. How will we/do we make decisions about who does what?
5. How will we/do we make decisions about finances and making purchases for the business?
6. How will we know when we're successful?
7. How will/should we be compensated for working in the business?
8. How will we/do we find time for ourselves as individuals outside of the business and our relationship/family?
9. How will we/do we structure our business, so it's fair, equitable and beneficial to our family and us? E.g. equal partners in a partnership, both directors of a company, having the business in one partner's name and 'employing' the other etc.

Note: You may need the advice of a professional if you don't know the answer to or need more clarity on question 9 – either a lawyer, accountant or financial advisor, depending on your circumstances/needs, should be able to help.

Conscious Business Coupling Contract

A more formalised step to putting a concrete shared vision into place is the creation of a Conscious Business Coupling Contract.

While this may not suit or be necessary for all couples, it does provide a level of confidence, understanding and clarity to both partners once you agree on your shared vision.

I've created a simple contract template you can use, customise and edit to best suit your needs. You can access it via the 'Book Bonus' link below: **www.blossomingbusiness.com.au/mmb-bonus/**

If you choose to put a Conscious Business Coupling Contract in place, use it for the purpose in which it's intended – your shared vision. See and appreciate its value in drawing you together for a shared outcome, guiding the way so you can concentrate on the steps you need to take to achieve your vision.

But also be conscious of its requirement to be kept up to date. Visions can change and shift, particularly when your relationship as a couple evolves.

In her book *Couples That Work*, author Jennifer Petriglieri writes about the different stages of a couple's relationship, and that there are three distinct stages or transitions that happen through the course of your life as a couple. Transitions that occur when going from a carefree couple to becoming parents, from significant changes to work conditions/career or business success levels through to becoming empty-nesters and questioning what's next.

Thus, your Conscious Business Coupling Contract should be reviewed or updated whenever a significant change happens within your business or relationship to ensure you're both on the same conscious business page.

The 'Mr & Mrs' in 'Mr & Mrs Business'

You've probably gathered by now that I like to ask questions. So here's another for you. Did you get married or become partners to start a business? My guess is you didn't, and your marriage or 'coupling' came first.

It's easy to get lost in your business and take for granted the relationship that brought you together before your business was even a twinkle in your eye.

In Section 3, we discuss the importance of self-care for both of you as individuals and how to support each other as a couple.

But it's important to note that in all of the work you choose to embark on together in business, there's no greater work you can do than on your relationship with each other - the Mr & Mrs in your business.

So before we move into the more practical and action-oriented parts of the book, I want to take a moment and allow you to consider your relationship.

Is your business more important than your relationship? If yes, I think you need a different kind of book than the one you're reading now.

If your answer is no, then I can confirm this is the right book for you. And you're about to read the most important piece of advice I'll give you in this book. It's in bold below, just to reinforce its importance.

Your business is not more important than your relationship.

Please keep this in mind as you work through the book and use it as a reminder while making decisions and changes from the information provided.

Start with the Fundamentals

Couples have a unique set of demands on them when building a business together. To achieve success without stress you, therefore, need a unique set of fundamentals that help you meet those demands.

As a couple in business, if you don't put these fundamentals in place, you won't have the strong structure necessary to work together. Ideally, you would plan these when starting in business, but they can also be used for an established business. It's never too late to steady the structure!

I've mentioned a few of our fundamentals already, but here's a list of what I consider the non-negotiables when setting up or revising your business as a couple:

1. Values
2. Shared Vision
3. Business Structure and Operation
4. Logistics of Living and Working Together
5. Boundaries
6. How to Find Time for Yourself and Your Needs

Before we define each of the fundamentals, it's important to note that the focus of Mr & Mrs Business is not how to build all of the fundamentals (we do cover some) but on managing the top three stressors for couples in business.

If you feel you have work to do in getting the six fundamentals in place, there are resource suggestions provided to point you in the right direction.

It's absolutely worth the investment in time to get these in place and build a strong structure. These will hold up your business and relationship for the long term.

1. Values

Values are your very personal, deeply held views of how things should be, how you see the world and how you live your life. They are your core beliefs.

They play out in your daily life, relationships and work. They form how you react to things, how you do things, who you align with, what you like and dislike, and how you feel.

You can have different values as a couple – we're all unique - but you both must agree and act on the values that relate to your business.

This fundamental will form an important part of how you do business together.

Take some time to understand and discuss your values and the values you want to work by in your business. These will also be an important part of forming your shared vision in fundamental two.

The Mr & Mrs Business Tip on page 33 of this chapter helps you explore your values further.

2. Shared Vision

While writing this book, I did some research within several Facebook groups for couples in business. By far, the most common response to questions around why couples in business struggle was a lack of shared vision.

You need to have a shared vision to work towards and keep you on the same path to your future as a couple in business.

Earlier in this chapter, we discussed creating your shared vision, and you may have formalised this in writing using the Conscious Business Coupling Contract or your version of one. The next step with your shared vision is to create a business plan and set goals.

Business planning and goal setting are tools to keep you, your business and your staff on the same path to success.

Business planning is a big-picture view of your business, both now and in the future. There are many ways to create a business plan, from complex business plan documents down to a simple Excel spreadsheet.

Choosing what tool to use will depend on your business needs and the result you want. For example, a new business may be more focused on creating sales and a customer base. In this case, the business may start small with a spreadsheet and some sales projection figures. Business planning and goal setting may come once the business is up and running, with a shared vision as the initial guide.

Setting goals becomes essential in achieving results once you have a plan in place. Goals get you where you want to be as per your business plan/shared vision.

As with your shared vision, when setting goals for your business, do this together and review as often as applicable for your business. Quarterly and annual reviews of goals and plans are an excellent place to start.

Business goals also give you a great reason to celebrate your successes together.

3. Business Structure & Operation

Below are some examples of what your business operations should consist of. Some of these we will cover in greater detail in the Time and Money sections.

- A visual business structure using an organisational chart or similar. Even if some of the roles are vacant, or you and your partner are doing some or all of those roles right now, drawing a visual representation helps set the intention for your future structure as you grow.
- Have clearly defined responsibilities in the form of job descriptions (see page 117 for more information).
- Written or recorded processes for everyday tasks that allow anyone in your business or new employees to learn how you do things. This is a huge time-saving tool both in the time you save training staff and in creating efficient and consistent task completion.
- Have good money management systems in place, e.g. bookkeeper, online accounting system and regular access to up-to-date reports on the status of your business, including cash flow to allow you to make informed business decisions.

- Have an efficient business system, including processes mentioned above, plus systems for storing documents digitally and shared online access so you have one source of truth for business information.
- Good money monitoring - know where your money is going and when it's not coming in on time.
- Ongoing productivity assessments, including identifying when to outsource and delegate to remove time/money intensive tasks from your business operations.

More information on business operations topics can be found on our website both on the blog and via our newsletter. To visit the blog or sign up to the *Grow Your Business* newsletter visit:
www.blossomingbusiness.com.au

4. Logistics of Living and Working Together

There is no guidebook for what works when balancing the responsibilities of your relationship/family and your business. There are many variables, and they won't all relate to your particular circumstances as a couple in business. However, here are some examples to get you thinking:

- Will you need day care/after-school care for your children?
- Who's responsible for pick up and drop off? How does that affect working hours?
- How do you manage household duties if both of you work full-time hours?
- How will you take holidays from your business as a family/couple?

5. Boundaries

Boundaries are not created to fence you in. They're built to set you free! Setting boundaries is essential for any couple in business. Without them, you'll develop bad habits, accept things you normally wouldn't and end up with no line between work and home.

The stress created by a lack of boundaries has no place in a business run by a couple. We will cover how to set boundaries in Chapter 6.

6. How to Find Time for Yourself and Your Needs

Living and working together is a lot. It can drain the closest of couples.

How you carve out time to each pursue your own hobbies and interests outside of the business, and your relationship/family is important. It relieves stress and allows you the space to be someone other than a wife, husband, partner, mother, father, and business owner.

Having time for yourself outside of your business and relationship is healthy and provides opportunities for self-discovery and great awareness of your own needs.

We'll delve into Self-Care and finding time for yourself in Section 3.

Communication

You may have noticed that communication is not one of the six fundamentals. This is a deliberate decision to highlight communication as a key part of being a couple in business (and a couple, full stop).

Communication in and of itself is enough for a whole other book. Every one of the six fundamentals in this chapter requires you to communicate as a couple to create them, and to keep communicating as your business grows.

If you feel communication is an area that may hinder your success, particularly around the topics of Money, Time and Self-Care that we'll be working on in this book, you should as a priority find ways to enhance your communication as a couple.

This could include counselling, coaching or starting simply by doing some research together on the topic and discussing. Even a quick Google search, reading through some couples communication articles and discussing things you could implement together from what you find is a good first step to take.

Do what works for you but don't avoid it. Communication problems will quickly undermine any work you do and derail your best-laid plans for success as a couple in business.

Tools in This Book to Help Your Communication

1. The Mr & Mrs Business Couples Quiz, which is located at the end of this book was created to support and encourage opening your communication as a couple before you work through the book.

I recommend you stop reading here, head to page 141 and complete the Mr & Mrs Business Couples Quiz before moving on to Section 1: Money.

2. Each chapter ends with a notes section to encourage you to write reminders of things to discuss with your partner, topics you'd like to explore further or things to take action on.

In Summary

Putting the fundamentals in place gives you something substantial to build on. It's the makings of a profitable and sustainable business.

They also give you the stability to grow and expand your business without adding stress, burning out and affecting your relationships with each other and your family and friends.

Take some time to review the six fundamentals and to do the work to ensure they provide the structure for your business and your relationships to thrive.

Mr & Mrs Business Tip:
There are some great free resources for uncovering your values available online. A simple Google search for 'defining your values' returns over 182 million results.

It's valuable (pun intended) knowledge to have as individuals and as business owners.

Knowing your core values and those of your partner will be a great help in understanding what makes each other tick and why you do the things you do. They underpin how you go about daily life without you even realising it.

Do some Google research and find a values assessment tool to try or complete the Values Exercise in your 'Book Bonuses' found at
www.blossomingbusiness.com.au/mmb-bonus

Summary of Foundations Chapter

- Conscious Business Coupling
- The Mr & Mrs in Mr & Mrs Business
- Start with the Fundamentals

Mr & Mrs Business Foundations Chapter Notes

To discuss with your partner/things to action in your business

SECTION 1
MONEY

CHAPTER 1

Your Money Status

Understanding your current money status can be a daunting process if you've never looked at it before or you've been avoiding it altogether.

And like many of us, you've likely been raised not to discuss money or spend too much time thinking about or focusing on money.

Some of the common beliefs many of us will have heard growing up can still affect our ability to deal with money today, often subconsciously limiting us or affecting how we think of money.

Sayings like: 'Money is the root of all evil', 'Money doesn't grow on trees', 'Time is money', 'One man's loss is another man's gain', and 'Beggars can't be choosers'. You get the picture.

So it's no surprise money is one of the largest contributors to stress in business and life. As a couple in business dealing with business and home/life finances, you've twice as much to stress you out.

It's a sensitive topic for many people, but it's critical you discuss it as a couple. And we need to pull the bandaid off by starting with your personal finances as a couple or family.

Before we move into your business finances in the next chapter, there needs to be a clear and mutual understanding of the status of your personal finances. For most couples in business, your personal finances and expenses are reliant on your business.

If you're in control of your personal finances, then your business won't hold as much money pressure and stress to 'provide' for you. You'll know exactly how much you need as a family, and you can plan accordingly.

For couples starting a business together, knowing the status of your personal finances is an excellent tool for making conscious decisions. You know going into business together how much you need as a couple to cover your bills and living expenses, and you can be realistic about your money status when you start your business and work out how you're going to meet your personal financial commitments.

This is important knowledge if both of your earnings are reliant on your business. You may need to question if this is even possible in the first year or two because if it isn't, stress will soon appear in your business and home life.

Knowing your money status, understanding your personal cash flow, having a personal/family budget and managing your bills are four key areas to becoming financially happy.

In the following section, the Personal Finances Exercise will help you uncover your money status. While we don't cover cash flow, budgeting and bills management, I would encourage you to do some work on these areas as a couple to reduce the money stress on your relationship.

You can also head over to the 'Money' section on our blog for more information on these topics: **www.blossomingbusiness.com.au/blog/**

Where Is Our Money Going?

If 'Where is our money going?' is a commonly asked question in your household, then you're not alone.

You're one of many everyday couples around the world who have a blurry view of their current money status.

As a numbers person, I love using statistics to put things into perspective. So let's take a look at some statistics related to money:

- As of 2016, Australia's total personal debt was around $2 trillion, and the average Australian household owed $250,000.
- The Australian Bureau of Statistics (2019) reports: 'Close to three in four (73%) households were in debt in 2017–18. Of these households, 28% were servicing a total debt that was three or more times their annualised disposable income.'

- A survey of 1001 Australians by online financial services company Spaceship found '38% of people said they don't feel comfortable talking about finances with their partner', while '60% admitted to feeling stressed about their bank accounts' (Spaceship 2019).
- AMP's *Financial Wellness Report* advises that '2.44 million Australians are suffering from financial stress' with the earnings bracket most likely to feel financial stress between '$50,000 and $74,999'(AMP 2019).

What these statistics confirm is we can't afford to ignore money. The more we use and manage our money online, the easier it becomes to 'set and forget'. We very rarely enter a bank, and it's predicted by as early as 2022 Australia will be cashless, depending on what online statistics you believe.

Credit is easily accessible for a large part of our population, with no-interest loans and interest-free periods, credit increases, and delayed payment options found online at the click of a button. This ease of debt creation can create a false sense of financial status. The hidden reality of how much interest you're paying and the amount of debt you have can easily be misinterpreted.

To know where your money is going and how much debt you have, you need to see the full picture. To reduce the money stress or pressure you feel about your personal finances, you need to feel in control of it and set it up in a way that works for your family while helping you achieve your goals.

From personal experience, I know once you sit down and get clear on what you have and what you owe, you'll see that whatever your situation, it's possible to make changes that will reduce the stress money holds over you. You may even feel a sense of satisfaction and enjoyment in working out your true money status. This means you're on your way to being financially happy!

Money Analysis

Before you start the Personal Finances Exercise, I want to make you aware of some things that are important in avoiding the stress that money conversations can create in relationships - business or otherwise.

1. Gaining knowledge and clarity are the primary reasons for doing this exercise.
2. If money usually triggers arguments or tension for you as a couple, go into this exercise with an open mind and clear, honest communication. This is not a test to find the person who spends the most money or to assign blame over your money status.
3. Most couples have a 'money person' in the relationship, who generally takes on a large part of the responsibilities for handling and managing money. Whatever the outcome of this exercise, this isn't to find fault with your current money managing system. It's a clarity exercise.
4. If you don't have a clear separation between personal and business finances, just do the best you can to get some clarity. (We'll discuss the importance of having separate personal and business finances in Chapter 2.)

Some advice on when to do this exercise

Do not do this exercise when:

- you've had a stressful day in your business (particularly if stressed by issues around money)
- either you or your partner is sick, unmotivated, tired, or emotional
- you have limited time (better completed as much in one sitting as possible – trust me, once you start, you'll want to know the outcome).

Do this exercise:

- with a clear space in time of an hour or two without unnecessary interruptions
- during business hours when you can call your bank or financial institution if you need information, e.g. your interest rate
- preferably with your partner or with your partner contactable to answer questions you may need to complete the exercise.

How to complete the Personal Finances Exercise

1. Take a piece of paper and pen or start a new spreadsheet. (See example in Table 1.)
2. Enter all of the banks/credit cards/financial institutions you use or have debt/loans with, as well as debts to people, businesses and the government such as tax debt, PAYG, and student loans.
3. Create columns for:
   - Card Limit/Total Loan
   - Amount Owing (as of today)
   - Interest Rate, if applicable
   - Payout Date (if a fixed-term loan or interest-free periods apply)
   - Minimum Repayment Amount required
   - Amount you are paying (may be different to the minimum)

- Date of week/month you make repayments
- Payment Regularity (e.g. weekly, monthly)

4. Total up the amount owing column.

	Card Limit/ Total Loan	Amount Owing	Interest Rate	Payout Date	Mimimum Repayment	Amount You Are Paying	Date of Week/ Month You Make Repayments	Payment Regularity
X Bank Credit Card	$5000	$3200	21%	20/10/20	$99	$120	Fridays	Weekly
X Bank Loan	$10000	$8000	9%	10/08/22	$180	$180	10th	Monthly
Bank								
Other								

Table 1: Example only

Stepping into Change

You now have the full picture of your current money status. It's an empowering feeling to see your money status in its entirety and know you can take control and make a change.

You don't have to look hard to find examples of people who, even on a small income, have been able to take control of their finances by taking small steps. In his book *The Barefoot Investor*, Scott Pape (2017) has many such examples and is worth reading just for the inspiration!

Now you have an overview of your personal finances as of today, what do we do next?

If you've discovered from the results of this exercise that you need to make some changes to get 'financially happy', then you'll need to look in detail at your results and decide as a couple your first action step.

If you're already financially happy and under control with your personal finances, go you! Either skip ahead to Chapter 2 or keep reading to see if you pick up anything new.

When my husband and I did this exercise as a couple, years ago, it literally changed how we managed our money. And it was instrumental in how we successfully made our way through the money crisis created worldwide by COVID-19, still affecting millions of businesses as I write this book.

Having a very detailed up-to-date view of our money allowed us to reassess our finances when our business sales reduced almost overnight due to COVID-19. We knew exactly where we could pull back our expenses and most importantly, we didn't succumb to increased stress through this time. Our knowledge and clarity on our finances made the shift in priorities easily manageable.

In deciding on your first action step to make a change, you should consider what's viable for your family circumstances. From my own experience, looking at removing the smallest debt as quickly as possible, regardless of its interest rate (people commonly start with the highest interest rate item) is a good place to start. Decide what amount you can afford weekly to pay towards the smallest debt, while still making minimum repayments on any other debts, if relevant.

I know firsthand how powerful this is, and we've implemented it with great success in our family. The success of this simple strategy is found in the satisfaction and motivation of seeing a small debt paid off and moving on to the next one. We often stumble when we don't see results at the beginning of any change, so this strategy keeps motivation up, and you can see results quickly.

Consider setting up a recurring payment via your online bank account. This is a great way to pay off debt quickly. This 'set and forget' system of dealing with debt often means that without even realising it time flies, the debt gets paid off and you're on your way to making financial happiness a reality.

If time is going to fly, you may as well use it to your advantage!

In Summary

In this chapter, we looked at your personal money status, using an exercise to clarify the state of your personal finances.

We looked at the outcome and identified areas for you to explore in further detail with your partner, to decide on any required changes.

Mr & Mrs Business Tip:

If you don't have a money tracking system in place, a simple small step would be to use a budgeting and expense tracking app like Pocketbook. This type of app syncs with your bank accounts, loans and credit cards to allow you to categorise spending and see where your money is going at a more detailed level.

It's a free app and available from the App Store and Google Play.

Other options are:

- Goodbudget
- Wally
- Budget Tracker

Summary of Chapter 1

- Where Is Our Money Going?
- Money Analysis
- Stepping into Change

Mr & Mrs Business Chapter 1 Notes

To discuss with your partner/things to action in your business

CHAPTER 2

The Business of Money

Thinking back to when you started your business (or now if you're considering starting), what were/are the things you want to achieve?

Take a minute and write down two or three points.

Did making a profit/profitable business make it onto the list?

I hope so. Because I hate to state the obvious: to have a sustainable business, you need to make money. You also need to know if you're making money. If you aren't, you need to know if you can turn the situation around.

In this chapter, we look at the areas of your business finances you need to know well and look at regularly.

Our goal of success without stress is made more achievable by knowing your numbers.

When I first started my business, even though I'd been managing Profit and Loss Reports and million-dollar-plus budgets for over fifteen years in the corporate world, I didn't take the time to put the basic financial fundamentals in place.

And guess what happened? I didn't make money. But I also didn't know I wasn't making money. To regularly look at my finances wasn't on my to-do list. I was so busy creating and developing my business, that I failed to focus on the one thing that would allow me to stay in business – making money.

Fast forward to 2020, and now I have great money systems in place I can easily manage and which allow me to make informed business decisions. I can quickly draw reports and know the financial status of my business at any time. My sales and costs are up to date and reviewed every few days. But it took time and the creation of good money management habits to get here.

When I took control and put these systems in place a few years ago, I know you can guess what happened. I started making a profit and growing. Even though I felt silly for not putting in place something so obvious, it reminded me that sometimes the most obvious things are easily missed.

When you're busy creating a business or navigating a growth phase, you can miss or skip over things - the foundations you need to be across to support you in any stage of your business.

Let's take a look at the financial foundations you should know about in your business to feel comfortable, calm and in control, no matter what you find.

Where Is Our Profit Going?

It's easy to assume most business owners have a very good handle on where their money is, where it goes and how much they have.

But this isn't the reality. I've worked with many business owners who are so consumed working in their business that understanding their business finances is an 'I'll get to it' task for later, like tax time or when cash flow is low.

Does this sound like you? As a business owner, it's hard to have to manage all the different aspects of your business. And as a couple in business, you're both generally focussed on the tasks you each have taken responsibility for (or have the natural talent/experience for) in your business.

Unfortunately, this can allow problems to occur that can't be flagged ahead of time, and instead, you feel like you're fighting spot fires (or worse, bonfires) instead of fanning the flames of growth.

As a small business, you may not yet have a bookkeeper and accountant you trust enough (or can afford full time) to keep you across issues and make you aware before they become problems to fix.

Or if you do, you may rely on them to be across all of your finances which means you don't have the chance to have a good handle on your business finance status. While every business is different, there are some financial foundation areas you should keep a regular, if not daily, eye on.

Financial Purpose

In the Financial Purpose Table below, column 1 shows the financial foundations.

For each foundation, column 2 shows the purpose for monitoring them closely or how putting a system in place to manage them will help your business. Column 3 indicates how you can maximise them for efficiency.

FINANCIAL FOUNDATIONS	PURPOSE	MAXIMISE
Regular expenses (outgoings)	Save money	Review regularly
Regular payment dates	Save time	Automate
General running costs per week/month – 'keeping the doors open' cost	Manage cash flow	Documented
Profit & Loss Report (P&L)	Manage money, make informed decisions, save time	Automate
Debtors – outstanding and total invoices/sales	Manage cash flow, save time, reduce stress	Review regularly
Reconciling bank accounts for up to date cash flow status	Manage cash flow, save time, reduce stress	Complete daily
Bookkeeping management and systems in place	Save money and time	Systemise
Cost of each of your products/services to produce/supply	Manage profits, save money and time	Documented
Budgets/goals versus actual sales	Manage profits, growth and success, reduce stress	Automated

Table 2: Financial Purpose Table

Let's explore these foundations and get an understanding of your knowledge of them in your business, or if you're considering starting a business together, your knowledge of how to manage them in your future business.

Business Finances Analysis

This exercise is to help you understand the essential numbers knowledge you should have about your business. Answer honestly, as this is a step towards identifying areas of your business knowledge you can focus on learning more about after the exercise.

Our goal is to get you understanding and managing the financial foundations in your business to reduce any stress they're creating and avoid any stress they may create in the future.

How to Steps – Business Finances Analysis

On a scale of 1 to 5 (5 being highest, 1 being lowest), score your knowledge of each item listed below in your business. Use N/A if not relevant.

FINANCIAL FOUNDATIONS	SCORE
Regular expenses (outgoings)	
Regular payment dates	
General running costs per week/month – 'keeping the doors open' cost	
Profit & Loss Report (P&L)	
Debtors – outstanding and total invoices/sales	
Reconciling bills for up to date cash flow status	
Bookkeeping management and systems	
Cost of each of your products/services to produce/supply	
Budgets/goals versus actual sales	

Example Table 1: Business Finances Analysis

Highlight or circle any score that's between 1 and 3.

How to Take Action

You may find in completing the Business Finances Analysis that you have some financial foundations scoring 4 or 5 because you understand them or review these foundations regularly. That's great!

For any financial foundations that scored between 1 and 3, you should view as an opportunity to spend some time expanding your knowledge.

All of the areas we looked at in Table 2 – The Financial Purpose table, can either save you time or money, better manage your money, help you make informed decisions or even reduce stress.

There are many resources and options available to business owners to delve into any of the financial foundations in greater detail.

A bookkeeper or accountant is an excellent place to start, particularly if you already have one you trust. They should be more than happy to spend some time going over these foundations, creating processes with you/for you or producing reports that give you a snapshot of the information you require regularly.

For further information on the items in the Financial Purpose table, access the 'Book Bonus' page at
www.blossomingbusiness.com.au/mmb-bonus

For our bookkeeping services, visit
www.blossomingbusiness.com.au/services/

In Summary

What have you discovered so far? Are there areas you identified in the Business Finances Analysis you can work on to make managing your business finances easier?

Even small changes to these areas can help reduce your money and business stress and allow you to make more informed and confident business decisions.

Mr & Mrs Business Tip:

A simple strategy to help you see where your money is going and build good money management habits is to keep your personal and business bank accounts separate.

Set up a Business Bank account and run all business-related transactions from this account, both sales (receipt of payment) and costs (expenses paid by business). Avoid paying for expenses with your personal accounts or credit cards, and if you do, pay this money back from your business account to allow it to be accounted for in your business costs.

Summary of Chapter 2

- Where Is Our Profit going?
- Business Finances Analysis
- How to Take Action

Mr & Mrs Business Chapter 2 Notes

To discuss with your partner/things to action in your business

SECTION 2
TIME

CHAPTER 3

Why Is There Never Enough Time?

In business and life, it can often seem like you're chasing time.

In 2016, when I started my business, I had one- and two-year-old children. Time was not in high supply! I made a lot of mistakes and worked far too many hours. But the biggest and most transformational lesson I learnt from the mistakes I made was around the use of time.

As a mum and one part of a couple building a business, I was always busy. I worked around my children's sleep and needs, and there was often nothing left in the tank for me or my husband. But I always felt like the light at the end of the tunnel was getting closer. If I just kept going, it would all fall into place and get easier.

But guess what? It didn't. The more I worked, the more there was to do. The later I worked and the longer the days, the less I achieved.

Until I realised there was a better way. I had to create time.

With fresh eyes, I decided to look closely at how I used my time. I found a lot of the tasks I was spending time on were not things I enjoyed doing or had a natural talent for. They also weren't creating revenue and could be done by others. Overall, I was losing a whole lot of energy—physically, emotionally and mentally—doing things that weren't necessary for me to spend time on.

As a creative person, I love doing anything that involves writing blogs, developing documents, creating social media posts, and website development. But these tasks don't directly make money for my business. They're investments, and the revenue they produce is, for the most part, unseen and unmeasurable. They're important in creating recognition for my brand, influencing the sales process and educating my audience, but they can also consume more time than the monetary outcomes they produce. I know this is my weak spot in my business, and I manage accordingly with a mix of time scheduling (because I still enjoy doing them) and outsourcing.

When I recognised this as a weak spot in my ability to be productive and profitable, it was a turning point in my business. Through identifying and taking action to change how I manage and prioritise my time, I created more freedom, less stress and my profits increased.

How to Identify Time Zappers

Before you can create time, you must work out what you're currently making time for and whether these things are important.

Have you ever noticed when you're enjoying something time melts away, and you're no longer conscious of it? You're no longer concerned by it. This is the ultimate zone of joy.

So what happens when you're doing something you don't enjoy? Does it feel like it's taking forever? Draining your energy and leaving you unmotivated to do the priorities on your to-do list?

This allows procrastination to step in, and suddenly it's taking longer to complete the task, using valuable time and energy you could have spent on other priorities.

These are time zappers. These are bad news for your business and life.

In a study by the Society for Personality Assessment, 40% of those surveyed reported they had experienced 'personal financial loss due to procrastination' (Edward Lowe Foundation 2020).

This is just one of the many reasons why identifying time zappers in your business is important. Some of the issues they cause include:

- leaky boundaries between work and home life
- stress and disorganisation
- longer hours and a constant feeling of being overworked
- resentment
- loss of energy and motivation.

Identifying the regular tasks that zap your time allows you to determine the ones you can reduce, remove or delegate to create time for your priorities.

This is particularly true of couples in start-up businesses using a DIY approach to their workload. It's normal for a business in the start-up or even growth mode to be unaware of the right time to delegate tasks to others within their business or to outsource.

When you do start to analyse tasks in your business, you'll soon find many can be:

- either reduced, streamlined or made more efficient through processes or automation
- removed if they don't add anything to your business
- delegated to others in your business (if you have staff) with the skill or ability to learn it or, by outsourcing to an expert who specialises in this task and thus does it faster and more efficiently. Note: having processes in place helps with delegation or outsourcing of tasks to others.

Time Analysis

When it comes to what you do on a daily/weekly basis – I know you're busy. No couple in business are twiddling their thumbs with time to spare. But I do know by taking some time to track your daily/weekly tasks we can find some things you can take off your plate to create more time.

Are you ready to see where your time goes? Great, let's do it, no time to waste!

How-to Steps: Tracking Your Time

Step 1:

Complete the Time Analysis on a sheet of paper or in a document by creating four columns.

Daily Business-Related Tasks	Weekly/Monthly Business-Related Tasks	Rating (1 to 5)	Reduce / Remove / Delegate

Table 3: Time Analysis

In the first column, write down all of the business-related tasks you do in a typical day.

In column two, repeat this with the business-related tasks you only do weekly/monthly.

Some examples as a reference are:
- Xero reconciling of bank account
- weekly client invoicing

- entering work hours into a tracking app
- daily Facebook posting to the business page.

Note: You can also do this as a separate exercise for your home-related tasks if you want to look at ways to create more time in your home life.

Step 2:

When your list is complete, use column three to rate each task in importance from 1 and 5 (5 being highest, 1 being lowest). *Tip: if you have any that you consider a zero, they've got to go now!*

To score each task, you need to decide based on the importance to your role - not the importance to the business. As an example, creating a P&L report is important to your business but is it important that you're the person who completes this task each week?

Ask yourself these questions for each task:
- Is it important **for** you to do it? i.e. no one else can do it
- Is it important **to** you to do it? i.e. you enjoy doing it

Step 3:

For any task with a score between 1 and 3, in the fourth column, write the appropriate possible action for the task. If you need to place two options against a task you can, but try to choose the one you feel is the best choice where possible:
- reduce
- remove
- delegate

For any task with a score of 4 or 5, you can now see what's important. However, it doesn't mean we can't streamline them further and create more time. (We'll get to that later in Chapter 4.)

What's Important?

Can you remember a time when you had to decide between fun and practicality? Or costly versus cheap? Or need versus want?

These are all examples of decisions made based on importance. And depending on where you are in life, who it's important to and what you need it for, you may have gone with either option. In other words, it's not always clear cut.

We take into account several things when deciding how important something is.

In the Time Analysis exercise, the importance of the tasks you scored as a 4 or 5 may be tied to you doing them due to your skill/talent and knowledge of the task or your desire to do them.

Equally important in deciding if they can more efficient is their importance to the success and outcomes needed by the business. The next chapter will help you determine if it's time for a change to any of your important tasks.

In Summary

Long hours and never-ending to-do lists don't make for great work/life balance or great relationships. They create stress and leave you unmotivated, emotional and cranky.

Knowing how you spend your time is the first step in creating more time in your day and your business. Choosing a few key things to understand, evaluate and change is the next step.

Mr & Mrs Business Tip:
If you want to get a formal or quantitative analysis of where your time goes, there are time tracking apps and websites that can help you (and your team). There are many free options or free trials to get you started. Here are a few – all with different options and abilities:

- Toggl
- Clockify
- My Hours

Summary of Chapter 3

- How to Identify Time Zappers
- Time Analysis
- What's Important?

Mr & Mrs Business Chapter 3 Notes
To discuss with your partner/things to action in your business

CHAPTER 4

Time Poor to Time Rich

$\mathcal{B}$ eing time poor has become an unwanted side effect of working and living in today's world. Our access to an unprecedented amount of information, opportunity and technology has given us problems not seen in previous generations.

Problems like overworking, burnout, stress, exhaustion and mental health issues are becoming more common than ever before.

Along with money, time has increased the stress on business owners significantly. In fact, the World Health Organization (WHO 2019) says, 'Burnout has become so prevalent among modern workers that it's now classified as an occupational phenomenon.'

As a business owner and part of a couple in business, I know you feel like you are up against some pretty significant time issues.

But here's the thing - we all are. Every single one of us has only twenty-four hours in a day. And we both know out there in the greater business world there are people just like you and I kicking time goals. Getting stuff done. Creating time. #itspossible.

Before we take a look at how to find ways you can kick some time goals, let's remind ourselves of why we want more time.

Why Do We Want More Time?

Try this simple exercise. In the section below (or on a sheet of paper) write down three to five things you would do if you had an extra two hours in your workday each week.

1. _____

2. _____

3. _____

4. _____

5. _____

Now write down a few words to describe how you would feel if you were able to get these things done? e.g. relieved, less stressed, excited

_____

The benefits of creating time in your business and life are many. As a reminder, when you take the time to create time, you get:

- space to dream, breathe, think and plan within your business
- a sense of fulfilment in getting things done in your day

- more quality time with your family (without the usual stress and guilt)
- time to be more creative, inventive and innovative in your business
- time for your self-care and self-development
- ability to focus on what you like to do in your business - the things you went into business to do/create/be
- time to enjoy your business and being in business as a couple
- time to build your business strategically
- success without stress.

Efficiency and Productivity

Knowing what you spend your time on is a great starting point for creating more time and increasing your productivity.

In Chapter 3, you completed the exercise on time zappers and worked out what's important. In this chapter, we'll look at some of the ways you can introduce efficiencies using this information.

But first, what exactly is efficiency, and how can we improve it? I consider efficiency as doing tasks that need to be done in a shorter amount of time, in a more organised way - taking the fastest route to get something done while still achieving the best result possible. The benefit of efficiency is productivity, an essential ingredient for a profitable business.

Being efficient and productive with my time comes easily to me. It's a skill I've built and honed over many years in corporate roles, where productivity was essential. Early on in my career, I rose quickly into management positions and took on large workloads, finding myself in many sink or swim moments.

When I reflect on how I worked through times like this, an organised approach to managing time, tasks and making decisions was always my starting point. Setting up systems to create a common, logical structure, and finding and fixing efficiency gaps were the foundations.

And as I came to discover, these were also the key foundations in creating success without stress. So let's get some of my efficiency and productivity to 'virtually' rub off on you!

Here are three tips for increasing your productivity by managing your time, tasks and decision making:

1. Decision Making

Making decisions in business and life can be great time zappers and make you less productive. So being able to make decisions fast when necessary is essential.

Decisions require consideration of their importance and the possible outcome.

- How important is this decision to my vision/results for my business and/or life?
- What will it do/create/provide for my business and/or life?

These two questions help you prioritise the importance of a decision with a clear understanding of the facts. Emotion or feeling should be removed, which can blur your clarity and decision-making ability.

When you don't have the time to think over a decision (clear your head), you should use the facts and the level of importance as your guide.

Having clarity on your shared vision, as discussed in the Foundations Chapter, will also help you consider the importance of a decision concerning the goals of your business. It allows you to be laser-focused on what's really important and what's of lesser significance.

2. Multitasking

Multitasking is commonly deemed as something women do well. I believe that viewing multitasking as a skill or something to aspire to do well is pressure women just don't need.

To be efficient, we need to think about multitasking differently. The expectation of multitasking is getting many things done, but how well are they done? Multitasking can create a false sense of efficiency and productivity if tasks are done just to finish them rather than on the outcome or quality of the result.

There have been countless studies that show the effect of switching between tasks and the impact on productivity. A study by Stanford University found 'heavy multitaskers were less mentally organised' (Verywell Mind 2020). To be effective, we need to focus.

If you think about it, focusing on more than one task at a time is impossible, because when you change tasks, you shift your attention. The effect of changing focus will impact negatively on productivity. When you change focus, you increase the risk of errors. You take longer to complete tasks and returning to do a different task takes time for your brain to reengage.

So how do we rethink multitasking when we have so much to do? The answer lies in a new approach to managing our to-do list. Instead of trying to fit all of our to-do lists into a day, we need to prioritise our essential tasks into the time we have available, with a focus on redirecting non-priorities into more efficient ways of managing them (reduce/remove/delegate).

Here's a peek inside my system:

As a working mum with a home-based business, each day (and week) is different, so my to-do list is fluid and continuously updated. I have a list of things in my calendar for the day, which is driven from Trello. I'm clear on the priorities (colour coding is great for this) and the things I'd 'like to get done'.

At the end of each day, I review the list and move anything to the coming days/week within a reasonable timeframe to complete them or meet a due date.

Things often drop off the list as I reprioritise. They may reappear later, be reassigned to be outsourced or disappear forever. Anything that starts to repeat is converted into a process.

Being efficient doesn't have to mean everything gets done every day - or done by you. Efficiency also means having a system. My business operations, systems and to-do list are all managed in Trello, which syncs to my calendar. Scheduling everything into Trello means I don't have multiple lists, ideas and projects written down. Each item can be stored, prioritised, and scheduled where relevant or even just parked for future reference and ease of finding.

My focus is always on knowing what's important, scheduling everything, putting my best into every task, being productive with my available time and being happy with the outcome.

Efficiency and productivity need a system to be effective. To find out more about using Trello, head to the *Grow Your Business* blog under 'Time Resources' here: **www.blossomingbusiness.com.au/blog/**

3. Fast Action

Success at anything requires taking action. Sitting on a decision, particularly in business, can lead to confusion, diminishing clarity and increasing levels of doubt. Not to mention, lost time and productivity.

Indecision can also be a sign of perfectionism or procrastination. Avoiding these productivity killers can be done by taking fast action when a decision needs to be made.

The two questions in Tip #1 on page 72 along with a quick assessment of the level of importance are the steps I use to make decisions. My decision might be 'yes, let's do it', 'no' or 'not yet' due to insufficient facts. But I act on the understanding of 'What's the worst that can happen?' If a mistake is made or the outcome is not what you expected, then you'll learn from it and enhance your ability to make similar decisions in the future.

In the fast-paced corporate arena, I had to get comfortable with making decisions, and acting quickly was a necessity. It takes time and focus to build up your action-taking muscle, but it's a great tool for any business owner.

Fast action won't work for every decision you have to make in your business. Some decisions require more thought, consideration and research. For those, absolutely take your time if you deem it worthy. Just make sure it's not perfectionism or procrastination in disguise!

Even the act of deciding if you can take fast action on a particular decision is a step in the right direction. The more fast action you take, the easier it will become.

Take Time to Create Time

Decision making, managing your time and tasks, and taking fast action are all efficiency tools. They help you make changes and improve productivity. But change also takes time.

Are you ready to commit to the time needed to create time? I know it sounds like an oxymoron. But the reality is you're going to need to spend some of your already scarce time on this for it to work.

Think back to the exercise at the beginning of this chapter about how you'll spend your extra time, and the benefits to you of creating time. Use this as motivation to commit some time to create time.

Efficiency Review — How to Create Time

In Chapter 3 on page 62, your Time Analysis gave you scores of importance for the tasks you complete in a day.

If you didn't complete the Time Analysis, go back and finish it now. I know you're going to want to create some time in your day/week!

Creating Time with Tasks That Scored Between 1 to 3:

Using your completed Time Analysis, look at the tasks you scored 1, 2 or 3.

These were tasks that aren't particularly important to you or for you to do. As they scored low in importance, your next question should now be:

- Is it important to the business that the task gets done? i.e. your business results/success relies on its completion.

Let's take a closer look at your less important tasks and the three options you used in the last chapter to categorise them – remove, reduce and delegate.

Remove

Surprisingly, you may come across some things that just aren't important to you or your business success. These are your 'remove' labelled tasks. Feel free to action those as soon as possible. These are your first and immediate time creators!

Reduce

Next, let's tackle the 'reduce' labelled tasks. These tasks are still important to your business, but you identified they could be reduced, streamlined or made more efficient through a process.

These are the tasks to create processes for once you've made your way through the book. You can get help writing processes in the 'Book Bonus' section of the website: **www.blossomingbusiness.com.au/mmb-bonus**

Delegate

Lastly, there's the 'delegate' label. Now here's an excellent time creator.

Is there anything on the list you can delegate NOW without training or with a few minimal instructions? NOW as in stop reading this book and email someone in your team (if you have one) and advise them from now on they can take on XYZ. Great, another one bites the dust – your second time creator!

Of the tasks left labelled 'delegate', are they relevant to outsource to external people or could internal staff (if you have them) be trained?

Depending on your level of urgency to create more time, decide what to do/who to refer these tasks to and when.

Take action within the next few days. Time awaits you - literally.

Creating Time with Tasks That Scored 4 and 5:

Once again using your completed Time Analysis look at the tasks you scored 4 or 5. There are two options for these important tasks.
1. Keep as they are, given their level of importance to you.
2. Check for efficiency gaps. View them with fresh eyes and see if you can identify weaknesses or parts of the task that could be enhanced.

For example, if you scored a 5 on the weekly report creation in your business, look at ways to automate that report. Xero has a report customising system where you can save the report as a template and run it every week at the click of a button. Time created!

It's possible to create time, even on tasks of high importance.

Creating time provides opportunities for continuous improvement in your business. Always look for ways to create time by regularly reviewing your tasks and asking the question – 'Can I do this more efficiently?'

What Do Successful Business Owners Do to Create Time?

Here are some of the common efficiency practices successful business owners use. They:

- have processes for every task in their business
- batch common tasks
- simplify their tasks and business
- automate part or all of their everyday tasks
- refine their systems and how they do things
- outsource tasks which are outside their zone of genius
- invest in systems, equipment and software where the money spent is worth the time it creates.

There are many examples of entrepreneurs talking about how they make their business efficient using streamlining, simplifying and even self-care. Here are two of my favourites:

In her book *Chillpreneur*, Denise Duffield-Thomas (2019) outlines many ways to be more efficient in your business and how she herself simplifies her home life to support her business life and vice versa. Her advice is golden, and some of her gems include having a keyless car and house, phone chargers in every room, choosing not to use voicemail or read emails and much more. Denise is the ultimate example of a 'Chillpreneur' in business and life.

Another entrepreneur leading the way in helping find time to do more of what you love in your business is Kate Northrup. Kate started as a money expert with her first book *Money: A Love Story* (2013) (which is an excellent money mindset book), and now focuses on time and energy management for women in business. In her book Do Less Kate shares a fresh perspective on time management strategies such as time-bending (sounds weird but it totally makes sense when you read it), as well as fourteen 'Do Less' experiments that really get you thinking about how you use time.

Slip-ups and Meltdowns

Implementing the tools, strategies and suggestions I've provided you within this book won't give you immunity to the stresses of time. Life as a couple in business is a rollercoaster of highs and lows, as it is in any business.

You will slip-up. You may meltdown. But don't give up. As well as the time strategies shared in this chapter, there are some additional things you can do to help keep you on track as your business evolves and changes, or when time takes over.

1. Timeout

If you find yourself regularly taking on stress due to time, consider finding a 'timeout' practice. It's important to step away, even for short periods, if you recognise your stress level rising.

Slowing down due to stress caused by time may seem impossible, but you cannot work under pressure for prolonged periods. Think of stress as your mind and your body giving you signals to slow down.

Here are some examples to help you step away and recharge:

- Breathe. Taking a few deep breaths can get you out of a lot of stressful moments and will slow down time long enough for you to get back on track.
- Spend time outdoors – walk around the block, go to the local park and read a book, head to the beach if you're lucky enough to live near one.
- Find a local yoga or meditation class or do some research into relaxation exercises you can use in the moment to calm you down.

2. Review your business and your systems regularly

Six monthly reviews are a good place to start. A lot can change in six months, so implementing the strategies in this book then going back to business as usual will soon find you back where you started.

Your review should include looking at your current time zappers for any new efficiency gaps. You can do this using the Time Analysis, and review the last analysis completed as a guide. If you feel a lot has changed, complete a new analysis of your daily/weekly tasks.

How to Recognise a Time Review Is Needed in Your Business

Some significant events that could affect your time as your business grows and indicate a review is necessary are:

- hiring new staff – induction, training, working with them until they can work autonomously
- an increase in business – delivering sales/services and managing the growth
- new products/services – selling, training, educating your market
- a downturn in business – needing to find new clients/customers/ business direction.

You can also use the below as a sign you should review your time:

- an increase in your levels of stress
- an increase in your working hours/days

Your business is ever evolving and changing, so your methods of creating time need to do the same. You may just need a few tweaks after a review, or you may need to create a new process, or outsource more/ different work or remove things from your business that no longer serve a purpose.

Choose what will work for your business and circumstances. Just don't ignore the time and stress signals and continue until something dramatic brings you back to reality.

Stress is not good for your health or your business! We're about to cover this in more detail in Section 3: Self-Care.

In Summary

In this chapter, we explored ways to create time and improve efficiency and productivity in your business.

Going from time poor to time rich.

Implementing even some of these tips will set you on the path to the ultimate goal of being time rich and you should have now identified areas you can get started on in your business.

You need to make time to create time.

Mr & Mrs Business Tip:
We talked about creating time by delegation and outsourcing in this chapter. But before you can do this, you need to know how to pass the responsibility for tasks over to someone else. The most effective way to do this is to create a process.

Writing down what you do is one way to create a process, but a great time-saving tip is first to record yourself doing the task.

For any computer-based tasks you complete, you can use a system like 'Screencastify' that records your screen as you do the task. You can then either convert it to a written process or use it as a training video.

'Screencastify' does require a Google account and runs via a Google extension, so you also need to use Chrome as your internet browser. It's free to set up an account and use it to record up to five-minute videos, which it autosaves to your Google drive. Alternatively, you can upgrade for an annual fee for longer recording time (US$49 per year at the time of writing).

Summary of Chapter 4

- Efficiency and Productivity
- Take Time to Create Time
- Slip-Ups and Meltdowns

Mr & Mrs Business Chapter 4 Notes
To discuss with your partner/things to action in your business

SECTION 3
SELF-CARE

CHAPTER 5

The Self-Care Connection

*W*hy are we talking about self-care in a business book and what's the connection between the two?

In this chapter, we take a look at self-care, a tool not commonly discussed in business which, in my opinion, is a crucial piece of the puzzle when it comes to business success without stress.

If you aren't achieving all you want in your business, self-care is one of the tools that can help you get there.

Connecting Self-Care and Success

Let's start by explaining what I mean when I say self-care. Ignore the mainstream, wellness and popular versions of self-care you see in the media and the online world today. I don't want you to get the idea that I'm talking about getting a massage, sitting in the sun or walking in nature - although those things can be amazing to help your overall health and wellbeing.

I want to go deeper. I want you to understand the fundamentals of self-care that make it so important to success without stress as a couple. It's the things you need to know about yourself and your partner to really see the benefits of self-care.

Once you have this, what you choose to do and how you take action on adding self-care into your weekly routine will be clearer and more meaningful to you.

What is Self-Care?

Self-care centres around self-awareness.

It's your understanding of the unique way you function in the world around you.

It's your appreciation of your skills and how best to use them.

It's knowing how to care for yourself to ensure you put your best foot forward in business and life.

Self-care helps you stay aligned with your values, and feel fulfilled within yourself, your business and your life. It reduces stress, promotes health and wellbeing and provides new levels of personal understanding and mental clarity.

Do you see the connection between practising self-care and running a business as a couple? Self-care gives you the tools to bring the best version of you into your business and your relationship as a couple.

It must be part of the business conversation. And for couples in business, it's crucial to your success.

Self-Care in Your Business

Business owners with successful sustainable businesses have a high level of self-awareness and understand the importance of caring for themselves in order to be successful.

If you follow the entrepreneur Jack Delosa's work, his journey in business has been full of high's and low's. Still, he's built a business that's sustainable for the long term, and he teaches other entrepreneurs how to do the same via 'The Entourage'. He lives his life with a good balance of business savvy and self-care. He gets the importance of working on yourself as hard as you work on your business and doing what you love and what fulfils you. You can read more about this and his views on inventing a better tomorrow for yourself and your business in his book *Unwritten* (2016).

Stress and Self-Care

The Australian Psychological Society (2020) describes stress as 'feeling overloaded, wound-up, tense and worried, and occurs when we face a situation we feel we can't cope with'.

There are two types of stress as business owners you may experience – acute and chronic.

Acute is the short-term stresses that can happen many times throughout the day, and they don't stay around for long. Generally, as humans, we cope well with acute stress as it's part of everyday life and work, so we recover and move on. Tasks like finishing a report that's due, dealing with a difficult customer, the last day of a job that you're pushing to finish on time, are all examples of acute stress.

Chronic stress is a stress that stays with you for long periods, e.g. continually working long hours, ongoing cash flow issues and relationship problems. This type of stress doesn't give you time to recover as it's continuous; stress levels rise, and they stay high.

According to a survey of small business owners conducted by mental health advocacy group Everymind (2017), 57% of small business owners report above-average stress levels.

Reducing your stress levels through self-care is essential to both your health and your ability to bring your best to your business.

Let's look at how as a couple in business you can take the lead in using self-care as a strategy for success without stress, right alongside your money and time strategies.

Defining Success

Self-care is based on self-awareness. A very practical step in building on your self-awareness is to define your meaning of success, as individuals and as a couple. This is valuable information in developing meaningful self-care strategies.

Define Success Exercise

Ask the question in bold below and either take some time to discuss it together, or on a notepad/paper, each writes down your answers and then discuss. You'll end up with a number of items on your list. There is no minimum or maximum.

Note this isn't about setting a money goal to achieve success. Your definition of success may include physical items or be the achievement of living the abundant lifestyle you want for you and your family. But it's not about how much in dollar figures you want to earn. That's part of business sales strategy (not covered in this book), and money in dollar figures often has very little to do with what success will look and feel like to you.

So here's your question:

What does and doesn't success look like to you?

Here are some examples:

- Does it look like flexible hours to ensure you can pick up and drop off your children at school and spend time with them?
- Does it look like living in your dream house and living your dream lifestyle with your family?
- Does it look like a four-day week?

- Does it look like working from home?
- Does it look like an office with staff?
- Does it look like a business that makes you money while you travel, i.e. a location independent business?

Our aim in defining success is to see what's important to you and your partner. You may find you have some differing success markers.

For example, in doing this exercise if your partner says he or she really wants to work towards a four-day week and your idea of success is to finish at 2.30 pm every day to do the school pick up, then that's okay.

You're on the same page in that the hours you work (or not work) are important to you both. This is a shared understanding of how you'll both feel successful.

One of the early realisations I had about my definition of success was that it didn't look like late nights.

When I implemented the steps coming up in Chapter 6 around boundaries, I found a way to restructure and refine my work that didn't include working at night regularly. This allowed me time to do things I enjoy at night for my self-care and fulfilment rather than working.

Now I feel more productive with a clear, focused mind when working during the day, and I feel I've succeeded when I don't work at night and instead take time for self-care. When I act in accordance with my version of success then my business and relationships benefit.

Knowing what's important helps you see what you need in order to feel fulfilled and successful.

But what I really want you to get from this exercise is ways you can take care of yourself and your needs to feel successful and fulfilled, and ways to support your partner in their needs.

Introducing Self-Care into Your Routine

Your definitions of success from the last exercise may seem a long way off. Some of your definitions of success might require you to put some boundaries in place to achieve them, e.g. fewer work hours. (See Boundaries on page 111 for help with this.)

You can also use your definitions of success as a way to introduce self-care into your daily/weekly routine.

From the previous exercise on defining success, what stood out for you?

Choose the top one or two on your list and write down ideas on how you can convert them into a self-care activity or use the information to better support you in your working week to feel fulfilled and successful.

Here is an example:

- Success looks like living in my dream house in the countryside with my family and having an outdoor, healthy lifestyle.

If moving into your dream house is one of the ways you'll feel successful, then this is an excellent opportunity to focus on something that you're passionate about. Here are some ways you could use this information to better support your working week:

- Create a vision board or vision book with images of the house and how you would decorate the rooms.
- Have a favourite image of a dream house on your desk.
- Do some research on real estate or suburbs you'd like to live in or go to some open houses.
- Do an interior design course, if you have a passion for it, and can't wait to decorate the house.

These may at first seem like trivial things. You may ask how you'll fit any of this in (Section 2: Time helps with this one).

If it doesn't seem possible, you need to dial it back and start small. Experience the benefits and how it makes you feel before upgrading to one of these examples that take a bit more commitment. I understand this may be outside of your comfort zone or unlike anything you may have considered useful to your business and relationships.

So let's bring it back to the definition of self-care I gave at the beginning of this chapter.

It's your understanding of the unique way you function best in the world around you.

It's your appreciation of your skills and how best to use them.

It's knowing how to care for yourself to ensure you put your best foot forward in business and life.

Defining your success and using it as a tool for self-care gives you self-awareness on what's important to you. In the example above, doing things that bring you closer to and remind you of what's important to you (in this example your dream house and lifestyle) provides motivation, drive and encouragement to be the best you can be.

Making It Happen

The easiest way to ensure you take time for self-care is to schedule it as a repeating appointment in your calendar, just like you would any other task or important meeting or deadline. Create a habit by repeating it, and it will soon become your new normal.

Whether that's a regular Wednesday morning yoga class, finishing an hour earlier every Friday to focus on something important to you, or scheduling an hour a week to do an online course to develop a skill.

The key is it needs to be meaningful to you. It needs to be something that develops you, shows appreciation or a level of care to yourself and encourages you to put your best into your business and life.

It's also important to take time to recognise the benefits you get after you dedicate this time. Notice the feelings, motivation and energy it provides when you return to your work schedule. Use this as fuel and encouragement to keep doing it.

In Summary

In this chapter, we looked at the effect stress can have on you and your business and the connection between self-care and business success. Helping reduce some of the stress, alongside our money and time strategies, are self-care strategies.

The Defining Success Exercise provides a tool you can use to get to know yourself better and understand more about what's really important to you and your partner. This valuable information is just one of the ways you can introduce self-care into your routine.

Self-care is a crucial part of creating success without stress.

Mr & Mrs Business Tip:
Self-awareness can be explored in many ways, including mindset work, journaling, meditation, personal development, counselling, mentoring, books, courses, and much more.

You can also do personality testing via online questionnaires that provide a great insight into who you are, your strengths and default preferences. They're a great tool to develop a better insight into yourself, how you work and how you relate to others.

Here are some free options if you want to try this type of analysis. They can provide freakishly accurate results! To get insights that best reflect you, be honest in your answers. Don't overthink them or try to get the 'best result'.

www.16personalities.com/
www.crystalknows.com/personality-test
www.9types.com/newtest/
www.123test.com/personality-test/

Summary of Chapter 5

- Connecting Self-Care and Success
- Self-Care in Your Business
- Introducing Self-Care into Your Routine

Mr & Mrs Business Chapter 5 Notes

To discuss with your partner/things to action in your business

CHAPTER 6

Taking Care of Yourself and Each Other

You can't give the best of yourself when you're running on empty. As a business owner, wife, husband, parent, friend, son, daughter, mentor, manager, and so much more, you're relied upon by many people.

In order to be all you want to be in business, you must first make sure you're all you can be in your life on a physical, emotional, mental and spiritual level.

In the first 'version' of my business, I learnt this the hard way and looking back I don't know how I (or my husband) survived. During the first two years of my business, my hours were long - I thought I had to do this to create a successful business.

My two daughters were still in nappies, not sleeping through the night, and at that age, they needed me during the day. So the bulk of my work was done late at night after they went to bed or during their short daytime nap.

You can imagine how effective I was working on an empty tank, exhausted continuously and with no time to take care of myself. Autopilot was running the show, and my workload was managed by what I could fit into the time I had and what task required the least amount of energy. The decisions I was subconsciously making were based on being tired, not on the best outcome and needs of my business.

As a couple in business, you may or may not have children in the picture, but regardless this same scenario can creep up on you too. A lack of sleep, overworking and not taking care of yourself will slow you down and make you less productive. It's inevitable if you try to sustain this over long periods.

There may be busy periods in your business when it's all hands on deck and longer hours are required. You may have work that suits you better to complete at night or on weekends. Creative people often love late nights or early mornings. This isn't the kind of overworking and stressful workload I am talking about.

I'm referring to the unrealistic expectations we put on ourselves. The workload we take on and burn ourselves out with. There are better ways of running your business. Smarter ways of taking care of yourself so you can sustain the busy times and longer hours when needed.

The self-care foundations you put in ahead of time will serve you best when the busy times occur and allow you to no longer sacrifice efficiency and productivity.

We've looked at putting work into your money and time management. These foundational structures help steer you through busy times and prepare you for growth. This last section of the book is now about you.

Taking Care of Yourself

Making time to do things that grow and nourish you gives you the energy, mindset and attitude to show up as the best version of yourself in your business.

In my workday, I constantly reprioritise to ensure I'm not overcommitting, stretching myself too thin or compromising on time I have blocked out for things I need to do for me.

It's a habit I've built into my day over time and just one of the ways I take care of myself.

Your business and relationships deserve the best of you.

You deserve the gift of living the fulfilled and meaningful life you want for yourself and your family.

For some people, one of the hardest things to do is uncover what it is you really want or need to take care of yourself. Often we live our days on autopilot, surrounded by noise that can feel like we're being brainwashed into how to feel, and what to think, be and do.

Who Are You Outside of Your Business?

Have you been guilty of being consumed by your business? Are you feeling this now? I know I have on many occasions.

Choosing to run a business as a couple or a family means it's highly personal to you. Some may even refer to their business as their 'other child'.

You put your all into your business, like an artist tending to their creative works. It's your creation or something you've had a hand in creating and building together. It's your source of income, your way to feed, clothe, house and provide for your family.

Your business is about your future. The future you're building for your family.

So it's absolutely possible to get lost in your business and forget you're a person outside of what you do.

Each of us have things we've forgotten, left behind or ignored because we became too busy. Hobbies, sports, creative talents we once loved doing.

When left unexplored, they can give you an empty, 'somethings missing' feeling - the type you can't quite put your finger on. They keep niggling at you in the background, reminding you they still exist. They're waiting for you to rediscover them.

When I was emerging from my motherhood bubble and realised I wouldn't be returning to my corporate career, I felt a sense of loss for a lifestyle and the job I had loved. I knew the hours and travel of my previous role wouldn't work with motherhood. Initially, I ignored this and tried to return to work, but the universe had other plans, and it was a disaster. It didn't work.

I threw myself into building a business with my husband, which, as you heard in the introduction, did not go so well the first time around. When my consultancy was up and running, and things were finally starting to blossom, I had the feeling there was something missing.

My instincts told me to look back at my childhood for inspiration. What I found was something I'd stopped doing in early adulthood as I focused on life, travel and work — my creativity. I couldn't believe I'd left behind something I was so passionate about. I'd even considered making a career out of my creativity before the corporate world drew me in and kept me enthralled for the best part of twenty years.

Since that discovery, I've embraced my creative side once again. It is always part of my week and my self-care. It helps me be something outside of my business. And I have two young girls who continuously inspire me with their creativity. They encourage my need to be creative every day.

So who are you outside of your business? Are there talents, passions, hobbies, or sports you left behind when you started your business/ family/relationship?

It might be time to rediscover them.

What Lights You Up?

When you're consumed by business, relationships, parenting and everything else life throws at you, it's normal to push your own needs to the side for a while. It happens to all of us, whether in fleeting moments or long periods.

However, if you want to thrive in business and life, and achieve success without stress, you need to spend some time understanding who you are outside of your business and your relationships.

Below is a two-part exercise you can each use to uncover some of your hidden or buried interests.

Part 1: Reminiscing

Take a pen and paper and write a list of activities/hobbies you often did as a child. Reminisce about your childhood and focus on the happy times of play and the common themes/activities.

Repeat this as a teenager, and if you want to, as an adult.

Circle anything that brings up memories of passion, talent, joy and excitement.

Part 2: Play

Choose three to five things off the list that you could do now.

Over the next seven days, schedule some time to try out these activities.

Our goal here is to test what brings out the best in you and lights you up.

You can keep a journal or just take note of any feelings or realisations you have during or after the activity. Look out for anything that makes you lose track of time.

At the end of the week, review the activities that energised you the most or gave you a sense of fulfilment.

How did they affect other areas of your life? Some things to look out for:
- Did it make you happier and calmer at home?
- Were you able to deal with problems with greater clarity and ease?
- Did you feel a sense of renewed passion for life, business or even your relationship?
- Did you find some insights into who you are and what you enjoy outside of your business and relationships?
- Did you uncover something you would like to continue doing for your self-care?

Use this information. Add it to your self-awareness toolkit. You now know a little more about the unique ways you function best and how to take care of yourself in order to put your best foot forward in business and life.

Keep Exploring You!

If you want to delve further into self-discovery, here are six more ideas to explore:
- Do something you've always wanted to do.
- Do something you're nervous about doing.
- Let your inner creative out – paint, colouring-in, build something.

- Be curious — look at the world around you differently, explore it with new eyes.
- Revisit your childhood — reminisce with a friend or relative, and share stories.
- Act child-like — climb a tree, fly a kite.

Supporting Your Self-Care

As you spend more time on your self-care, it also strengthens your self-worth muscle.

You're acknowledging to your subconscious the value in having your needs met. You're recognising the importance of filling your cup first, so you're better able to help, serve, support and care for others.

Please don't underestimate the importance of this. If you fall back into old habits and ignore yourself for a while, just simply start again. Go back to basics and schedule time into your week.

Supporting your self-care is just as important as setting up good money and time management foundations. There are no foundations and no business without you.

Supporting Your Partners Self-Care

Equally important to your relationship as a couple in business is supporting your partners need for self-care. In doing these exercises together, you can understand and identify things your partner enjoys and encourage them to take time out of your business and your life together as a couple to explore them.

Ways you can support your partner include:

- holding them accountable to keep self-care activities in their schedule and showing up
- letting them know when they're acting outside of their own best interests and needs, health or otherwise
- encouraging them to work hours that align with their definition of success, where possible
- noticing and communicating how their acts of self-care are benefiting your business and your relationship
- consistently showing up for your self-care.

Taking Care of Each Other

Business can create a minefield of relationship issues for a couple. I've heard many couples say, 'It's not for everyone', or 'I could never work with my husband'.

While working together or even working in your own business may not be for everyone, I'm sure with a few key care-focused strategies in place that most couples could find a way to support each other as partners in business.

Let's look at what sort of care and support it takes to have a great chance at success without stress as a couple in business.

Why Boundaries Matter

Some years ago, I worked with a family-run business which gave me some valuable insight into how couples interact when operating a business together. The couple, we'll call them Mike and Amanda, had a number of areas, from my view as an outsider, that was undermining their ability to run their business and have a happy family life.

Mike worked out in the field, delivering their service while Amanda ran the office part time while also having a part-time job and managing their home and family.

Mike blamed Amanda for any problems from the office. And Amanda blamed Mike for any issues that happened in the field or customer complaints.

At their lowest point, Mike and Amanda were barely speaking at home or work, and this affected their employees and their business. Slowly over time, their problems made the business seem all too hard, and they decided to sell the business and Mike got a job.

After they decided to close their business, it took them a long time to recover from this experience and stop blaming each other and return to the relationship they had before they went into business together.

Besides not having the money and time foundations in place we've looked at already, one of the critical issues was their business had blended into their home life. They couldn't draw a line and see the boundary where work stopped and family began.

They lost the ability to communicate well, and they were struggling to give each other support, care and understanding.

They had shaky boundaries at best.

Identifying Boundaries

The definition of 'boundary' (Merriam-Webster Learner's Dictionary 2020) states, 'unofficial rules about what should not be done: limits that define acceptable behaviour'.

Boundaries are sometimes a scary word for people in business. It can seem like something that will fence you in, when in fact they set you free!

Setting boundaries is essential to successfully managing your stress around money and time and to help you stay focused on your self-care and your needs as a couple/family.

I know firsthand the freedom setting boundaries provides and I now use a number of boundaries to give me the space I need in all areas of my life. Here are some of mine:

- Work at night-time is rare.
- I don't answer my phone for work after 5.30 pm.
- I don't have my mobile phone in my bedroom when I go to sleep, and it has notifications set to silent between 9 pm and 6 am.
- Social media is limited to checking two to three times per day.

So how do you identify what areas of your life need boundaries?

Asking questions is a great way to help you discover a need for a boundary.

Try these:

- Do I resent doing this task?
- Do I have a clear line between business and home/family time?
- Do my children say I am always ...? (Fill in the dots, e.g. on the phone, scrolling on my phone, not listening, working, etc.)
- Does this task create stress for me?
- Do I feel anxious when this happens?
- Do I regret saying yes to this?

As a couple in business, one of the most important boundaries you can create is one that sets when you switch off from work. This boundary can take several forms depending on your family's needs, and can include:

- a time after which you no longer discuss work issues
- a time after which you no longer take phone calls
- a time after which you no longer do work
- a physical boundary after which you enter, work is no longer done/ discussed
- a timeframe/physical boundary during which you no longer think about work. This helps create space for you to be more present with your partner/family.

How To Spot a Need For a Boundary

The problem with deciding what needs a boundary is you often don't recognise it initially as 'unacceptable' behaviour. This can be due to limiting beliefs, a survival mode where you just make it through a busy workday on autopilot or existing under an unproductive workload disguised as busyness.

Limiting beliefs are ideals we've picked up from those around us, and subconsciously accepted as true. They can go right back to our childhood experiences.

Limiting beliefs are beliefs you hold to be true but are somehow limiting your potential. Most limiting beliefs are based on fear and can stop you from seeing areas that aren't serving you or your business well or need a boundary. Example: a fear of success, a fear of not finishing things, a fear of making money.

When you're in survival mode or working on autopilot, you may not see a way to stop doing some of the things you do by using a boundary. You may feel like it's better/easier to push through - it isn't.

When you're busy, you may believe that you're being effective and getting things done. But when you're busy and unproductive, then you have a false sense of achievement. A boundary can help remove some of the things that are stopping you from being productive.

Setting Boundaries

To help you see beyond your current circumstances in business, let's take a look at some of the boundaries that can make a difference for couples in business.

As you read through these examples, identify/circle those which relate to you as a couple.

1. Work/Home Life Boundaries

Creating a clear boundary between when work stops, and home life begins.

1.1 Time Boundary

Example: We don't work after 5.30 pm Monday to Friday. Weekend work is limited to Saturday mornings between 10 am and 12 noon, and/or Sunday afternoon between 1 pm and 4 pm.

1.2 Location Boundary

Example: Once we leave the office and enter the house (enter the <insert room> if you are home-based), work is no longer to be discussed.

1.3 Business Talk Boundary

Example: We don't talk business between 5.30 pm and 8 pm while we cook dinner, have family time and put the children to bed.

2. Client Boundaries

Create a line that you don't allow to be 'crossed' by clients.

2.1 Client Time

Example: We don't answer the phone or respond to emails or texts from clients outside 9 am and 5.30 pm.

2.2 Client Money

Example: We don't do any additional work for clients who have an invoice that is more than one month overdue.

2.3 Client Work Hours

Example: We only do client work Monday to Thursday. Fridays are our operations, communication and self-care day.

3. Communication Boundaries

It's imperative you don't blur the communication lines between you as a couple.

3.1 Respect Boundary

Example: We won't take our frustrations in business out on each other.

3.2 Listening Boundary

Example: Neither partner is more important, and we each have a role to play in the success of the business. We listen to each other's opinions and choose the right approach, no matter whose idea it is.

3.3 Clarity Boundary

Example: We have clearly stated written job descriptions, and we understand what each other brings to the business (see next section for more detail on job descriptions).

Many other boundaries are important both in business and as a couple in business. These are a starting point based on the common frustrations I've witnessed.

Which ones stand out for you as relevant to your partnership? It's vital to discuss them and find a way to action those you need in your business and relationship.

Putting them in writing is a great first step, as is advising others around you to keep you both accountable (your children and employees are great for this).

Appreciating Each Other's Roles

One of the first things I want to know from any couple in business I work with is, 'Do you understand each other's roles in the business?'

Appreciation starts with a very clear understanding of what each other's role and responsibilities are. If you can't articulate your partner's role and responsibilities in the business—or you know they can't articulate yours—the following exercise will help you fix this and put a formal document in place.

Each partner in a couple in business should have a clearly defined, written job description. This removes doubt, provides clarity and forms security around the importance of each partner's commitment to the business.

Even for couples where the business is built around one partner's skill/ expertise, the other partner is equally important in their role. You have both made a personal, future-focused commitment to create a successful business for your family.

A job description provides each partners role with clarity on the day-to-day responsibilities and is used to ensure the business is functioning well and efficiently. It also allows each partner to have input into their responsibilities based on their skill and expertise, rather than the duties that need to be fulfilled in the business structure.

You can establish gaps in a skill that can either be filled with one partner taking training or by employing or outsourcing that part of the business requirement.

One of the self-care fundamentals is appreciating your skills and how best to use them. Anyone who works outside of their skill and expertise is taking on the stress of feeling out of control and incapable. It opens the door to mistakes and is unproductive for business, affecting time spent and ultimately costing your business.

A job description is also a safeguard against blame, resentfulness, and disagreements over results between couples, providing a protective barrier to help support your relationship inside your business.

How To Create a Job Description

Before creating job descriptions, discuss as a couple a list of duties and responsibilities so you're both on the same page. Discuss your skills and area's you don't feel comfortable being responsible for.

When you're ready to create the job description, you can use your template, or download our template and follow the simple instructions from the 'Book Bonus' page on our website: **www.blossomingbusiness.com.au/mmb-bonus**

Acknowledge Each Other's Role

Now you each have a job description; the final important part of this exercise is acknowledging each other's responsibilities.

Go out for coffee, remove yourselves from the everyday of your business and sit down and read over the job descriptions together.

Discuss them. Here are some prompts you could use:

- Are you proud of and grateful for the abilities your partner brings to the business?
- Do you see the importance of each other's contributions to the business?
- Do you realise this would be a different business if you replaced your partner's role with someone who was an employee in your business rather than a stakeholder dedicated to the success of your business?

These prompts will help you to build and recognise the need for appreciation, an essential part of communicating as a couple in business.

Support, Care and Understanding

Support, care and understanding are all ways you can show your appreciation. But it also requires knowledge and communication.

We've looked at ways you can take care of each other by setting boundaries and understanding each other's roles in the business. But how do we show we appreciate each other?

Consistently and authentically. Consciously and honestly.

Some simple ways you can support and appreciate each other are:

- celebrating success together – making time to do this whether it's a small gesture, congratulations, or a more formal celebration like a night out or drinks
- thanking each other – you know when each other has gone above and beyond for your business (or if you didn't before you will now you understand each other's roles better)

- backing each other up – it's important, especially when you have employees, to show support for your partner and back each other up. Decisions for the busines always come from a place of bettering the business, even if it results in a problem to solve. Having each other's back is imperative to a good outcome for your business
- understanding each other's needs – inside and outside of the business, including the need to have time out to pursue other interest and have time for self-care
- respecting boundaries – committing to and actioning the boundaries that you've both set or if they can't be met, adjusting them or agreeing on a temporary boundary break by communicating
- being present – showing up in your couple/family time as passionately as you do in your business time. Being present and shutting down your work brain before stepping into your family/couple time. (Dr Adam Fraser has a great book on this called *The Third Space* (2012))
- loving each other – nurturing your relationship outside of the business, i.e. your 'us' before you were in business together. Making time to spend time together outside of work as often as is possible for your circumstances. Working on your relationship as a couple without the business helps you be successful as a couple within the business.

In Summary

Taking care of yourself and each other is more than self-care days and saying thank you every once in a while. It requires some crucial foundational work such as boundaries, understanding each other's roles and excellent communication.

It needs you to really take time to appreciate your needs, as well as your partners, inside and outside of your business. If you're not taking care of yourselves and your relationship, your business will not get the best of you.

Mr & Mrs Business Tip:
Create a success date night. Set a weekly/monthly date where you specifically celebrate success in your business.

Agree on the reason for celebrating prior and discuss it on your date. Find ways to complement each other on your involvement in the success of this particular result. Enjoy your successes together!

Summary of Chapter 6
- Setting Boundaries
- Appreciating Each Other's Roles
- Support, Care and Understanding

Mr & Mrs Business Chapter 6 Notes
To discuss with your partner/things to action in your business

Your Future As Mr & Mrs Business

Your relationship with yourself and each other is more important than your business.

For the majority of couples in business, you were a couple before you were in business together.

At least part of your vision for your future in business together should include enjoying it and being successful. Achieving this takes consistent work and action, like any relationship.

Take a minute to feel proud, grateful and appreciative of each other. Because reading this book means you're seeking out ways to achieve your vision as a couple in business.

Building a business together is something to celebrate and to be acknowledged. You're creating something wonderful for your future.

Congratulations on taking a step forward for yourself, your partner and your business. I'm honoured you've allowed me to play a small part in bringing your vision to life.

In this book, we've covered money, time and self-care, the three most common stress-inducing factors for couples in business.

Section 1 looked at your personal and business finances, how to understand them and create changes to manage them better.

In Section 2, we explored how managing your time more efficiently creates space to focus on the important parts of your business, relieving the pressure of always feeling like there is more to do.

And Section 3 was all about you and your needs as part of a couple in business. When you take the time to work on who you are outside of the business, you benefit from the increased energy, motivation and focus to work inside your business with more joy, efficiency and clarity.

Most couples in business are building something for their future. They have a long-term view of creating a successful, profitable business that will provide well for them and their family.

But the reality of business success is harsh. Many businesses don't make it past three years and one of our three key topics in this book is often the cause — money. That alone should be enough motivation to focus on growing your knowledge around your business and finances.

Being a couple in business creates a new curveball to your business success. It requires a conscious effort (like reading this book and taking some action) to work together on creating the business success you have in your sights.

If you look around you, there are couples in business successfully balancing their relationship and family with running a business together.

This is absolutely possible for you too.

I hope I've achieved my goal in writing this book, which is to help you recognise the important job managing your money, time and self-care play in creating success without stress as a couple in business.

If you're reading this book as a couple wondering if you should start a business together, this book is your test. Once you work through the exercises, if you feel more confident that it's for you, then take the next step towards your future as Mr & Mrs Business.

If you're reading this book as a couple already in business, choose what resonated most with you (or what triggered you the most) and start taking action in your business there. Start small and choose one or two things to work on improving together and see some success before moving on to any more changes.

The Action Checklist on page 127 will help get you on your way to success without stress as a couple in business.

I'm truly excited for you both and wish you every success for your future as Mr & Mrs Business.

Sonja

P.S. If you haven't already, don't forget to complete the Mr & Mrs Business Couples Quiz at the back of this book.

Get access to your 'Book Bonuses' here:
www.blossomingbusiness.com.au/mmb-bonus

Want to stay in touch? Let's connect online. You'll find my socials on page 140 or via my website

Action Checklist

Use this checklist as a summary and next steps guide

Page	Item	Tick When Complete	Write Any Business Actions Required
22	Conscious Business Coupling Questions		
23	Conscious Business Coupling Contract		
33	Values Exercise		
42	Personal Finances Exercise		
52	Business Finances Analysis		
62	Time Analysis		
70	Why We Want More Time Exercise		
76	Efficiency Review		
93	Define Success Exercise		
106	What Lights You Up Exercise		
113	Setting Boundaries Exercise		
117	Create a Job Description		

Additional Resources

Online

Your book bonuses, including the downloadable versions of some of the exercises in this book, can be found on the 'Book Bonuses' page on my website:

www.blossomingbusiness.com.au/mmb-bonus

The *Grow Your Business* blog has articles and information on growing your business:

www.blossomingbusiness.com.au/blog/

Books

I am an avid reader of books — okay, I'll confess to having a book obsession. Here are some of my favourites for business owners on the topics covered in this book:

Money:

The Barefoot Investor by Scott Pape

You Are a Badass at Making Money by Jen Sincero

Think and Grow Rich by Napoleon Hill

The Little Money Bible by Stuart Wilde

Get Rich, Lucky Bitch! by Denise Duffield-Thomas

Mindful Money by Canna Campbell

Time:

Do Less by Kate Northrup

The ONE Thing by Jay Papasan, Gary Keller

The E-Myth by Michael E. Gerber

Chillpreneur by Denise Duffield-Thomas

Self-Care:

The Art of Extreme Self-Care by Cheryl Richardson

The Muse Is In: An Owner's Manual to Your Creativity by Jill Badonsky

The Book of Self-Care by Mary Beth Janssen

The Path Made Clear by Oprah Winfrey

Help if you Need It

Mental health is a serious issue for business owners. If you're overwhelmed and need assistance from a professional, the following organisations provide support and advice:

Beyond Blue

Phone 1300 22 4636 (AUS)

Lifeline

Phone 13 11 14 (AUS)

Headsup

Employers can gain ideas and assistance in providing better mental health in the workplace. **www.headsup.org.au**

References

Introduction

1. Sensis 2019, Australian small business owners struggle in silence with stress and anxiety, Melbourne, viewed 17 June 2020, <https://www.sensis.com.au/australian-small-business-owners-struggle-in-silence-with-stress-and-anxiety>

2. Australian Small Business and Family Enterprise Ombudsman 2019, *Small Business Counts; Small Business in the Australian Economy*, Sydney, viewed 21 January 2020, <https://www.asbfeo.gov.au/sites/default/files/documents/ASBFEO-small-business-counts2019.pdf>

3. Australian Bureau of Statistics 2020, 8165.0 – Counts of Australian Businesses, including Entries and Exits, June 2015 to June 2019, Canberra, viewed 21 January 2020, <https://www.abs.gov.au/ausstats/abs@.nsf/mf/8165.0>

Foundations Chapter: Couples in Business

4. Petriglieri, J 2019, *Couples That Work*, Penguin Life, UK

Chapter 1 – Your Money Status

5. Australian Bureau of Statistics 2019, 6523.0 – Household Income and Wealth, Australia, 2017-18, Canberra, viewed 27 January 2020, <https://www.abs.gov.au/ausstats/abs@.nsf/mf/6523.0>
6. Spaceship 2019, Seven million Aussies losing sleep over money, Sydney, viewed 18 June 2020, <https://www.spaceshipinvest.com.au/press/article/spaceship-media-release-25-11-2019>
7. AMP 2019, Financial stress costing businesses billions, Sydney, viewed 16 June 2020, <https://corporate.amp.com.au/newsroom/2019/january/financial-stress-costs-businesses-billions-in-lost-revenue#:~:text=According%20to%20the%20report%2C%20there,per%20year%20in%20lost%20revenue.>
8. Pape, S 2017, *The Barefoot Investor*, John Wiley & Sons, Milton

Chapter 3 – Why Is There Never Enough Time?

9. Edward Lowe Foundation 2020, Stop Procrastinating, Michigan, viewed 14 June 2020, <https://edwardlowe.org/stop-procrastinating/>

Chapter 4 – Time Poor to Time Rich

10. World Health Organisation 2019, Burn-out an 'occupational phenomenon' International Classification of Diseases, Geneva, viewed 14 June 2020, <https://www.who.int/mental_health/evidence/burn-out/en/>

11. Verywell Mind 2020, How Multitasking Affects Productivity and Brain Health, New York, viewed 14 June 2020, <https://www.verywellmind.com/multitasking-2795003>

12. Duffield-Thomas, D 2019, *Chillpreneur: The New Rules for Creating Success, Freedom, and Abundance on Your Terms*, Hay House, UK

13. Northrup, K 2013, *Money: A Love Story: Untangles Your Financial Woes and Create the Life You Really Want*, Hay House, UK

14. Northrup, K 2019, *Do Less: A Revolutionary Approach to Time and Energy Management for Ambitious Women*, Hay House, UK

Chapter 5 – The Self-Care Connection

15. Delosa, J 2016, *Unwritten: Reinvent Tomorrow*, The Entourage Publishing, Simon & Schuster, Melbourne

16. Australian Psychological Society 2020, Stress, Flinders Lane, viewed 16 June 2020, <https://www.psychology.org.au/for-the-public/Psychology-Topics/Stress>

17. Everymind 2017, *Can digital interventions help to improve mental health and reduce mental ill-health in small businesses?*, Sydney, viewed 17 June 2020, <https://everymind.imgix.net/assets/Uploads/PDF/Small-business/SmallBusinessWhitepaperFINAL.PDF>

Chapter 6 – Taking Care of Yourself & Each Other

18. Merriam-Webster 2020, Learner's Dictionary, Springfield, viewed 18 June 2020, <https://www.learnersdictionary.com/definition/boundary>

19. Fraser, A 2012, *The Third Space*, Random House Australia, Melbourne

Acknowledgements

The biggest acknowledgement is for my husband, John. Thank you for always supporting me and my ideas (and mostly agreeing with them!). Never will there be a better Mr to my Mrs, in business and life.

I'd like to recognise and thank all of the clients who have allowed me into their businesses, trusted me, taken my advice, given me insight into their pain and shared with me their successes. I am grateful to have played a small part in helping your businesses blossom.

To my family and friends who I know are always there supporting me in anything I do, thank you. If you're reading this and are my family or friend, then I mean you!

Thank you to those people who've made this book possible - my cousin Georgia for helping me get organised, getting this book out into the world and for doing the promotional work behind the scenes. Tash, my forever supporter, best friend and the first person I trusted to read a draft of the book (after John of course). Emma Franklin-Bell for getting me started on this book-writing journey; your professionalism and advice is priceless. The talented Emma Veiga-Malta for creating the book cover and all of my branding, which perfectly combines my love of nature and helping businesses grow.

Finally, to my parents, my late father, Roger, and my wonderful mum, Cheryl, who always allowed me to feel like my many dreams were possible.

Author Q&A

Why did you write a book about couples in business?

I've seen firsthand how hard it is to be a couple in business, as well as experiencing it myself. The freedom, results and satisfaction that can come from getting it right are worth the effort to make the changes required. The topics I discuss in the book are strategies any couple can pick up, run with and make some changes.

Do you think every couple in business has experienced stress and frustration working with their partner in business?

Without a doubt! I'd be surprised if I could find any couple working together who doesn't have some level of stress around money, time and self-care.

Why are you so passionate about helping couples in business?

I love helping business owners. I find it extremely rewarding to see people find success in their business. When that success also helps their relationship, family and satisfaction in life, as it does with couples, I am beyond grateful for getting to be part of their journey. It is the most satisfying part of my job.

Often people have blocks around money and time, and they can find it hard to break through and make progress. What do you say to them?
Being a couple in business is a minefield of obstacles, where so many things could be set off at any time. The most common causes relate to money and time.

Having blocks around money and time are commonplace, no matter who you are - whether you're a business owner, employed or unemployed. My advice is to work on identifying your blocks first and take small steps to make mindset changes. Mindset work is so important, but that's a whole other topic (and book!).

What's your wish for people once they've read your book?
My heart aches for couples struggling to juggle business and life and feeling stressed every day.

My wish is anyone who reads this book will find some relief to their money and time stresses and find some time to build self-care into their week.

About the Author

In 2014, Sonja Balzarolo left her career after 20+ years in the corporate arena to have her first daughter.

Motherhood allowed Sonja to look at her career from a different perspective, and in 2016 she took a leap of faith and followed her dream of starting a business from home.

Sonja's business has changed and evolved into the bookkeeping and business consultancy - Blossoming Business. Through its evolution, one thing has remained constant - a love for helping business owners.

Blossoming Business focuses on providing, teaching and helping business owners create solid money foundations and efficient operational systems for growth.

Discovering the hard way how important it is as a home-based business owner to take care of yourself as well as your business and family, self-care has since become an integral part of Sonja's business strategy and the work she does with clients.

Sonja lives on the Gold Coast in Australia with her husband John and two daughters — Lily-Rose and LuLu Sparkle.

You can connect with Sonja in the following places:

Website: **www.blossomingbusiness.com.au**
Email: **sonja@blossomingbusiness.com.au**
Facebook, Instagram & Pinterest: **@blossomingbusiness**
LinkedIn: **Sonja Balzarolo**

The Mr & Mrs Business Couples Quiz

How much do you know about how your partner handles their money, time and self-care? Let's find out!

The Purpose of the Quiz

Being a couple in business can create stress, tension and resentment in your relationship. Frustration and blame can rear their ugly head.

Reading this book may also trigger you or your partner. While this is healthy, as it means you are identifying areas that need your attention, it may be a little uncomfortable.

For you both to start the book off in the right mindset, I've created this quiz as a light-hearted, fun but important way to identify gaps in your knowledge of each other. It will allow you both to be grateful and appreciate the talents, skills and experience you each bring to your business.

Getting Started

There are two versions of this quiz. Choose whichever one will work for you.

Option 1.   Complete the quiz on the following pages in the section relevant to you, i.e. Mr or Mrs.

Provide the book to your partner to complete their section (don't let them see your answers before they complete the questions).

Option 2.   Complete the quiz online using the link below. Both you and your partner can complete the quiz separately.

www.blossomingbusiness.com.au/mmb-quiz

Scoring Your Answers

You'll each need to mark your partner's quiz to provide the correct answers and calculate your score.

Tally the points by giving one point per correct answer.

Once you each have a score, refer to the scorecard and basic observations at the end of the quiz.

Mr & Mrs Business Tip:
Use the answers as a launching point to discuss how you both view each other in your business and how you both contribute to your business.

The quiz is an information and communication exercise. Any discussions on the results should be based on zero blame or judgement and done with appreciation and love.

The Mr Quiz

*Circle the answer that you feel is 'most like' **your partner** for each question.*

1. **How does your partner like to pay bills?**
   a. before the due date
   b. on the due date
   c. after the due date
   d. no idea

2. **What would your partner do if they won $200?**
   a. bank it/save it
   b. splurge on something for the family
   c. splurge on something for themselves
   d. pay a bill with it

3. **Does your partner:**
   a. love/like money
   b. hate/tolerate money
   c. have a love/hate relationship with money
   d. not even give a second thought to money either way

4. When attending an important event, is your partner more likely to:
   a. be late leaving home/arriving at the event
   b. be ready in plenty of time
   c. be right on schedule
   d. be unpredictable; anything could happen

5. Is your partner more likely to collect/organise important receipts by:
   a. always placing them in an agreed place, e.g. filing tray
   b. putting them in unknown places but eventually finding them
   c. leaving them wherever they fall in the house/car/office
   d. having no idea where they are

6. Which of the below statements is more likely to represent your partner?
   a. Time management is their middle name, and it's their superpower.
   b. Pretty good at managing their time to get things done.
   c. Always saying they never have enough time
   d. Oblivious to time.

7. When it comes to a hobby/activity they enjoy, is your partner most likely to:
   a. ensure they have time for their hobby/activity regularly
   b. try to do their hobby/activity, but it doesn't always happen
   c. talk about doing their hobby/activity, but it hasn't happened yet
   d. put everyone else's needs before their own or ignore the need for self-care altogether

8. **Your partner would most likely consider doing something they enjoy to be:**
    a. something they couldn't live without
    b. a nice thing to do when they can find the time
    c. a treat that will rarely happen
    d. not even a consideration

9. **Is your partner more likely to:**
    a. be very self-aware, know their own needs and what makes them tick
    b. be doing things now to better themselves and improve their self-awareness
    c. be curious about knowing more about themselves if they could or knew where to start
    d. take life at face value and not give themselves, who they are or what makes them tick much thought

The Mrs Quiz

*Circle the answer that you feel is 'most like' **your partner** for each question.*

1. **How does your partner like to pay bills?**
    a. before the due date
    b. on the due date
    c. after the due date
    d. no idea

2. What would your partner do if they won $200?

   a. bank it/save it

   b. splurge on something for the family

   c. splurge on something for themselves

   d. pay a bill with it

3. Does your partner:

   a. love/like money

   b. hate/tolerate money

   c. have a love/hate relationship with money

   d. not even give a second thought to money either way

4. When attending an important event, is your partner more likely to:

   a. be late leaving home/arriving at the event

   b. be ready in plenty of time

   c. be right on schedule

   d. be unpredictable; anything could happen

5. Is your partner more likely to collect/organise important receipts by:

   a. always placing them in an agreed place, e.g. filing tray

   b. putting them in unknown places but eventually finding them

   c. leaving them wherever they fall in the house/car/office

   d. having no idea where they are

6. Which of the below statements is more likely to represent your partner?

a. Time management is their middle name, and it's their superpower.

b. Pretty good at managing their time to get things done.

c. Always saying they never have enough time

d. Oblivious to time.

7. When it comes to a hobby/activity they enjoy, is your partner most likely to:

a. ensure they have time for their hobby/activity regularly

b. try to do their hobby/activity, but it doesn't always happen

c. talk about doing their hobby/activity, but it hasn't happened yet

d. put everyone else's needs before their own or ignore the need for self-care altogether

8. Your partner would most likely consider doing something they enjoy to be:

a. something they couldn't live without

b. a nice thing to do when they can find the time

c. a treat that will rarely happen

d. not even a consideration

9. Is your partner more likely to:

    a. be very self-aware, know their own needs and what makes them tick

    b. be doing things now to better themselves and improve their self-awareness

    c. be curious about knowing more about themselves if they could or knew where to start

    d. take life at face value and not give themselves, who they are or what makes them tick much thought

The Mr & Mrs Business Couples Quiz Scorecard

How did you go? Let's take a look at your scorecard and a basic observation.

MR SCORE: _____ MRS SCORE: _____

Note: Questions 1 to 3 focused on Section 1: Money, Questions 4 to 6 on Section 2: Time, and Questions 7 to 9 on Section 3: Self-Care.

Scores Between 1 & 3

Thanks for being honest! So your score looks low, but on the bright side, you're in the right place. Focus on communication and discussing the book as you go. Take this as an opportunity to get to know your partner well within your business relationship.

Scores Between 4 & 6

Great job! In some area's you have a good idea of how your partner deals with money, time and self-care. Take a look back over the answers that weren't correct. Do they fall into one section of money, time or self-care or were they spread out? This will give you an insight into what to look out for as you work through the book.

Scores Between 7 & 9

Well done! While this isn't a competition, your score is a good indication that you know your partner pretty well. But there're always new things to learn. Use the book as a discovery tool to uncover things you didn't know about your partner.

Additional Observation for All Scores

Take some time to go back and review your answers. Are there any in the 'c' or 'd' answer category? These are indicators of areas to work on within the topics of money, time and self-care.

For services and information on how to grow your business visit:

www.blossomingbusiness.com.au

www.ingramcontent.com/pod-product-compliance
Lightning Source LLC
Chambersburg PA
CBHW030523210326
41597CB00013B/1008